REACHING
TOWARD
HEAVEN

TEN STEPS FOR ACTIVELY
APPLYING FAITH TO
SOLVE DAILY PROBLEMS

CAROLYN RINGGER

REACHING

TOWARD

HEAVEN

TEN STEPS FOR ACTIVELY
APPLYING FAITH TO
SOLVE DAILY PROBLEMS

by

Carolyn Pearce Ringger

DEDICATION

To my wonderful parents, Don and Eileen Pearce, who are as kind, unselfish, and loving in the home as they are out of the home. Thank you for giving me life and unconditional love. They set the foundation for my deep doubting not faith in Jesus Christ.

To my husband, Hans, for being there to learn from and love.

To his parents, Louis and Hilde Ringger, for their strength, support, and happy humor.

To my brothers and sisters: Don, Lewis, LaReta, Cheryl, Scott, Aleta, Darryl, and Lynette for our joyful memories of life and the opportunity to learn to forgive one another in family life together.

To all of our extended family, including our nieces and nephews, for the good lives they live, which bring honor to our family.

To our children, Eric (and his wife, Kirsti), Kevin, Kent, Monica, and Hans for all of the love and beauty they have brought into our lives.

To my exceptional friends for taking the time to teach, support, and accept me.

Copyright © 1992 Carolyn Pearce Ringger
All Rights Reserved
Printed in the United States of America
Library of Congress Catalog Card Number: 92-070807
Covenant Communications, Inc.
Reaching Toward Heaven
Printed July 1992
94 95 96 97   10 9 8 7 6 5 4 3 2
Jacket Illustration by Simeen
Jacket Design by Leslie X. Goodman
ISBN 1-55503-391-1

CONTENTS

ACKNOWLEDGEMENTS

I AM GRATEFUL TO EACH PERSON WHO CONTRIBUTED TO THIS PROJECT AS it evolved into this new manuscript, *Reaching Toward Heaven: Ten Steps for Actively Applying Faith to Solve Daily Problems.* Among the many people who helped me as I wrote this book are Marguerite Dike, Ann Bennett, Elder Eberheard, and Elder Hamilton, who all had great desires to help; Elder Bush, Elder Hook, Elder Sergeant, Sister Johnson, and Sister Morgan, who were willing to put into practice the Ten Steps of Faith; and the many missionaries we taught to go forth in faith to find the elect of God. I also express my gratitude to President and Sister Woolsey for inviting me to share these steps throughout the Tempe, Arizona Mission.

I am indebted to Gertrude Smith who served as the writing editor of the first edition of this book: *Faith Unpuzzled.* She worked many long hours to organize and prepare that edition. I am also grateful to Arlene Bascom, the writing editor of this new edition. Working with her and Darla Isackson, editor at Covenant Communications, was a wonderful experience. Without our joint vision of what this material could do for others, this book could not have come forth.

Many of my family members and friends, both near and far caused me to have great courage in my life. I have included the names of some of these people because they are very important to me and so that they may know that they have meant much to me, in the past and the present, by helping me develop my faith. These people are Martha Johnson, Judy Naegle, Jill Homer, Lynn Morgan, Julie Himstreet, Bob and Rosemary Brown, Geri Harris, Joyce Hubbart Schultz, Joan Knight Norris, Linda Pearce Bell, Marva Stock, Diane Jensen, Mary Marsden, Sharon Bobo, Kay Reno, Muggins Shertzer, Karen Robinson, and my older sisters: LaReta Pearce Brinkerhoff and Cheryl Pearce Hatch. Others who have helped me grow in my faith include Claudia Sedgwick and her mother, my early-morning seminary teacher, with their ukulele music and love; Sisters Terrill, Marsden, and Briggs, some great adult leaders who are in my memories; and all of the girls of my camping days. To all those from southern California, Hawaii, Utah, Pennsylvania, and Arizona whose faces and names still flow in my memories: "Shalom." Other people who are important to me are all my Maori brothers and sisters; to them I send my love and greetings and say, "Pehea Ana Koi."

Vickie Awa and JoAnn Killmer, two of the best "shadow leaders" I have ever worked under, also deserve my gratitude. They deeply nurtured my use of faith and prayer when, at nineteen, I served as camp director in the Honolulu Stake. Others who helped me are Bunny Whitney, owner of the This Is the Place bookstore, located by the Washington Temple, and Mary Sturlaugson Eyer, author of *A Soul So Rebellious*, with whom I gave firesides in Arizona and California. These two women encouraged me to write and to share my insights.

Others I am grateful to are Kupi and Kathy Fitisumanu and their son, Michael, who treated me like a daughter and a sister, respectively, while I lived in TeAtatu, Auckland, New Zealand as a missionary; President C. Douglas Barnes, my mission president, who knew *how* to listen to the Spirit; and my mission companions, Sisters Brown, Meha, Brunn, Sund, Jones, Hare, Lyman, and Hanneman and the mission matron, Tia Wihongi, all of whom helped me increase my faith. I also express my thanks to someone I feel was one of the Lord's most special Apostles, LeGrand Richards, my father's mission president and mentor. My dad, Don Pearce, is much like that great man, so full of faith and love for people.

His influence upon my father has filled my cup as well. There could never be greater parents than Don and Eileen Pearce. Charity towards all is the way they have lived. I also express my gratitude to all of the great people for whom I have provided personal counseling. I have been blessed to watch their lives change as they have found success in using the information and steps discussed in this book.

Most especially, I desire to thank my husband, Hans, and our children, Eric, Kevin, Kent, Monica, and Hans L. for our family-life experiences, which caused the opening of my soul to learn how to make requests of and how to listen to the Spirit as I learned to be a better wife and mother.

Carolyn Ringger

FOREWARD

REACHING TOWARD HEAVEN IS A UNIQUE AND SPECIAL BOOK. Many books have been written on faith, a characteristic one needs in order to achieve a high quality of life. One reason this book is unique is its author, Carolyn Ringger. According to Carolyn, she grew up lacking confidence and experiencing many trials and problems. Lovingly and respectfully, I suggest that she fits the description Moroni gives to the humble followers of Christ: she is one of the "weak things become strong." (Ether 12:27.) Carolyn shares her hard earned understanding of faith in beautifully simple ways that are reminiscent of Nephi whose "soul delighteth in plainness unto [his] people, that they may learn." (2 Nephi 25:4.) From this book, you will learn much about faith that is plain, understandable, and inspiring!

Reaching Toward Heaven is also unique because of its "how to" formulas. I have worked as a student, a professor, and a counselor of human behavior for many years. All through history, we have searched for more effective ways to help people to learn and to change their lives for the better. More effectively than any volume I have seen in thirty years, *Reaching Toward Heaven* teaches us correct principles and how to apply these principles.

For example, mention New Year's resolutions in most groups and you will hear some chuckles. People react this way because such resolutions are not usually successful; however, they usually are good ideas. Most people who set New Year's resolutions do so with good intentions. But usually these resolutions are forgotten by February, if not before that. Why? Because the "how to" steps were not built into their goals to help them develop these good ideas, "line upon line," into real behaviors.

Reaching Toward Heaven truly gives us the precious gifts of plainly understandable examples of faith and clear and applicable steps that show us how to build a more faithful and happy life.

If you want to be more than inspired, if you want to truly experience a "mighty change" in your life, your marriage, your family, your ward, etc., read and follow the steps discussed in *Reaching Toward Heaven*.

The ideas found in Reaching Toward Heaven are more than theory. This book is a "Do-It-Yourself Owner's Manual" forged out of the refiner's fire of necessity, tested and proven to lift and heal your life with the help of God.

Brent Hinze, Ph.D.

INTRODUCTION

BECAUSE OF THE MANY HOURS I HAVE SPENT PONDERING LATTER-DAY prophecies, the Second Coming of Christ and the faith we need to prepare for it are uppermost in my mind.

What magnificent promises the Millennium holds for us! The scriptures tell us it will be a time of peace and joy because there will be no evil on the earth at that time.

Our leaders have told us that we will be the people who will live to usher in that event. If this is true, it must also be true that we are the generation who must learn to bind Satan. In my study, I have come to understand how this great binding of evil might occur. The purpose of this book is to share this understanding.

While I was still in my early teens, I was drawn to this area of study because I decided that I wanted to have peace and joy in my life. Often, during my high school years, I would wonder, "How will we bind Satan for the Millennium?" Whenever I ran into filth, I would ask myself, "How are we going to stop it? How will Satan be bound?" I studied scriptures on the topic at hand:

And Satan shall be bound, that he shall have no place in the hearts of the children of men. (D&C 45:55.)

For Satan shall be bound, and when he is loosed again he shall only reign for a little season, and then cometh the end of the earth. (D&C 43:31.)

How Will Satan Be Bound During the Millennium?

As an adult I came to understand the meaning of the word "heart" as it is used in the scriptures. Most often it means "thoughts in the mind." As I unpuzzled this word, a great spirit of comprehension swept over me and helped me understand how we will bind Satan. I was walking across the kitchen floor when the answer flashed into my mind: "It will be, in part, because we will listen to him no more in our *hearts* or our *thoughts!*" I remember standing in the middle of the room amazed at what I was finally understanding. *Individually, we can learn to bind Satan now!* My whole body was filled with joy at the knowledge.

Later, I read, "And because of the righteousness of his [Christ's] people, Satan has no power . . . over the hearts [thoughts/emotions] of the people, for they dwell in righteousness, and the Holy One of Israel reigneth." (1 Nephi 22:26.) We understand it will not be done with chains, but because we listen to him no more. (*The Millennial Messiah*, McConkie, p. 668.)

However, the *Doctrine and Covenants Student Manual 1985-86*, page 89, made me think harder on the subject.

> President Joseph Fielding Smith made these statements concerning the binding of Satan: 'There are many among us who teach that the binding of Satan will be merely the binding which those dwelling on the earth will place upon him by their refusal to hear his enticings. This is not so. He will not have the privilege during that period of time to tempt any man. (*Church History and Modern Revelation*, p. 192.)

Though these two statements may at first seem to be at variance, in reality they are not. It is true that Satan cannot exert power over men. The restrictions that will come upon Satan will be a result of two important actions by the Lord: (1) He will destroy telestial wickedness from the earth at his Second Coming; and (2) as a reward for heeding his counsels, the Lord will pour out his Spirit upon the righteous who remain on the earth to the extent that Satan's power will be neutralized—rendered totally ineffective. Thus, Satan will no longer have the power to tempt or negatively influence the Lord's people. Both the righteousness of the Saints and the operation of the Lord's power are necessary to bind Satan. If the Saints do not give heed to God's word, he will not impart of his Spirit; and if the Lord's influence is not brought to bear to aid the Saints, they, on their own power, will not be able to withstand the force of the adversary.

My greatest desire is that we can be among the righteous who are rewarded for "heeding his counsels" and looking forward to the Millennium when faith, instead of wickedness, will flood the land—when Satan shall be bound because we are filled with the Spirit and do not listen to him in our hearts or thoughts.

There is a direct relationship between our faith and our ability to bind Satan, and between our faith and our thoughts. We can control the thoughts that come into our minds. Controlling our thoughts will help us increase our faith. As we control our thoughts and become pure in heart, we grow in our ability to individually bind Satan; because of this ability, miracles will follow.

We have the power to:

1. Create our own thoughts.
2. Receive inspiration (or positive, uplifting thoughts from beings of light and truth).
3. Receive sinspiration (negative thoughts, from beings of darkness, that pull us down).

We can learn how to cancel the negative thoughts and input coming from Satan and receive the positive, pure, and enlightening information from the Lord.

We can individually bring about the binding of Satan when we eliminate our desire to do evil (See D&C 45:55). We can understand how evil input occurs, and learn to shut off such signals by refusing to receive them.

The Lord tells us in D&C 46:8-9 that he will give us great gifts to help us as we seek to keep the commandments; this obedience will help us become pure in heart. We will seek to discover what these gifts are and how to receive them.

My hope is that we can thereby begin building faith like unto Enoch's—faith which will eventually flood the land.

Enoch and a whole city became so pure in heart that they were of one heart and one mind and received all that they asked for. They became a Zion people. Is there any reason why we could not learn to do the same? The Lord needs a Zion people who are prepared to meet him at his Second Coming.

I think the people of Enoch must have decided as a group what their righteous desires and goals would be and then individually, and unitedly, presented their desires to the Lord. They were all willing to live for the blessings and to pray daily for them. They received those blessings both because they were consistent with the will of the Lord and because of their unwavering, undoubting, single-minded faith.

In one generation we have seen conditions degenerate from a basically good Christian value system in this society to widespread wickedness which overruns the whole earth. Nothing happens by accident. Satan has been working hard to bring this about. Now it is time for us to work hard to overcome the evil surrounding us. To do this, we must become of one mind and one heart, as did the people of Enoch, and start using our faith to achieve this goal.

The children of this generation have been told that because of their strength they have been saved to come forth upon the earth at this time, just before the Second Coming of Christ. I would also include their parents among the valiant ones who are to help prepare the earth for his coming. As parents, then, we must be prepared to teach our "Saturday's Warriors" so they can perform their special callings in these last days.

However, I am concerned as I see and hear of daily episodes in which Satan is winning. Instead of being valiant, some of our latter-day soldiers are joining the forces of evil.

The Lord has told the prophets to teach nothing but repentance. Why? Because when we repent we start the process of becoming pure in heart and only the pure in heart increase in faith and are powerful in actively applying it. I believe the Lord is waiting for us to awaken to the urgency of repenting and becoming pure in heart because only the pure in heart will be able to overcome the evil of these days, be allowed to see the Savior, and remain on the earth at the time of his Second Coming.

The key to faith, and thus the key to becoming pure in heart, is learning to monitor our thoughts and actions. When we have learned to do this, then we, as parents, will be armed to teach our children so they will have faith like unto the sons of Helaman. We must be trustworthy, as were the mothers of those 2,000 young men—young men who doubted not that their mothers knew God lives and that he would care for them and answer their prayers of faith. Would our children be able to doubt not and trust in our teachings as completely?

We must realize there is a pattern we can follow to receive the righteous desires of our hearts. We have stagnated long enough because of our lack of knowledge concerning faith. As we unpuzzle the laws of faith and learn how to use those laws and exercise our faith in Jesus Christ, we move from the first to the second principle of the gospel: repentance. As we repent, we become more pure in heart, and our faith increases, motivating more repentance. It is an exciting upward-moving spiral.

Therefore, verily, thus saith the Lord, let Zion rejoice, for this is Zion—THE PURE IN HEART; therefore, let Zion rejoice, while all the wicked shall mourn. (D&C 97:21.)

As we become pure in heart by repenting and purifying our lives, our ability to ask the Lord for the righteous desires of our hearts increases. Our faith can grow to the extent that we will be ready to set up a city of Zion, as did the people of Enoch. (Enoch's people were successful in doing so, even though there was wickedness around them, as is true of our situation today.)

We are not to be commanded in all things. It is time for us to use our moral agency in a way that will have a great effect upon our children. It is time for the righteous of our generation to learn to bind Satan, to teach our children, and to receive miracles, as did the people of the city of Enoch. Righteousness was established in that city even though the people were surrounded by wickedness, like we are today.

If we do not learn to bind Satan in our own lives, the wicked will overrun our families as the world becomes more and more wicked in the last days. We must learn to listen to Satan no more in our hearts.

The righteous can then be united and be of one heart and one mind to keep the evil which covers our land from overcoming us. We can also ask the Lord to inspire us individually to know what we can do to stand up and be counted on his side.

We and our children are as the armies of Helaman—we have been taught in our youth and we must be teaching our youth. As we purify ourselves we are like a sleeping giant, the Lord's army, who will awaken the powers of faith and overcome this world.

If not faith, what? If not us, who? If not now, when? It is time for good people to exert personal daily effort to increase faith until it begins to flood the earth as the gathering of the righteous takes place in these last days.

For whatsoever is born of God overcometh the world; and this is the victory that overcometh the world, *even* our faith. (1 John 5:4.)

Chapter One

LEARNING WHAT FAITH IS AND HOW IT WORKS

What Is Faith?

If you are like many of us, you are aware that faith is the first principle of the gospel, yet you may have wondered, "What is faith?"

You are familiar with the definition of faith which Paul gives in Hebrews 11:1, "Now faith is the substance of things hoped for, the evidence of things not seen." But the wording as given in the inspired version of the Bible, which Joseph Smith translated, clarifies this somewhat, as does the definition of faith given in Alma 32:21 in the Book of Mormon.

The inspired version of the Bible quotes it as follows: "Now faith is the assurance of things hoped for, the proof of things not seen."

Alma describes faith as follows: "Faith is not to have a perfect knowledge of things; therefore, if ye have faith ye hope for things which are not seen, which are true." If faith precedes the miracle, then what precedes faith? Your hopes and desires!

To Have Faith Ye Must Have Hope

Moroni 10:20 tells us that "if there must be faith there must also be hope." In Chapter 7 he says:

And again, my beloved brethren, I would speak unto you concerning hope. How is it that ye can attain unto faith, save ye shall have hope? (Moroni 7:40.)

As I read my scriptures, I began to see the words "hope" and "faith" on every page. I highlighted these words each time and like a path opening to my view I could see that the laws of faith were everywhere and whatever success I had experienced in solving my problems came because I had been using these laws. I realized that many people lose hope and faith because they place them on uncertain or worldly goals such as getting a certain job, marrying a certain person, or obtaining a certain degree of wealth. The scriptures taught me that I must place my faith and hope first on eternal realities (See Moroni 7:40-44). The scriptures began to feel like letters from home from a real Father. And his Son, Jesus Christ, began to feel more like my big brother who set a good example for me to follow. I began to see the scriptures also as additional "lectures on faith" or reports which show how others solved their problems by using the laws of faith as taught them by the Spirit.

Faith Creates All Miracles and Greatness in Our Lives

The Apostle Paul tells us in Hebrews 11:6, "But without faith it is impossible to please him: for he that cometh to God must believe that he is, and that he is a rewarder of them that diligently seek him."

This scripture used to feel negative to me. Then as I studied faith, I began to realize what the Lord is asking of us. He is waiting to help us. He wants to help us—if we will let him. But in order for Christ to help us, we must have faith in him and believe that he lives and that he *will* help us. The Lord can only help us as we ask and doubt not, which is the same as exercising faith. The Lord is pleased when we, by our faith, allow him to help us. D&C 67:1-3 tells us that fears in our hearts can keep us from receiving the blessings we ask for. Moroni 7:33 tells us, "And Christ hath said: If ye will have faith in me ye shall have power to do whatsoever thing is expedient in me."

In Mormon 9:21 there is a great promise given to those who develop the faith to ask and doubt not: "Behold, I say unto you that whoso believeth in Christ, doubting nothing, whatsoever he shall ask the Father in the name of Christ it shall be granted him; and this promise is unto all, even unto the ends of the earth."

D&C 46:30 clarifies: "He that asketh *in the Spirit* asketh according to the *will of God*; wherefore it is done even as he asketh." (Italics added.) So we avoid disillusionment and loss of faith by seeking wholeheartedly the will of God and asking in the right spirit for the right reasons. (See D&C 46:7-10.)

After studying and researching the subject, I can now describe what I see to be the meaning of faith, as it applies to faith in the Lord Jesus Christ, in the following statement: faith means that you believe in Jesus Christ, and that your inner self-talk and feeling about Christ are positive; you doubt not that he lives and that he can do all things. Let's put it another way:

1. When you know that Jesus Christ lives and you doubt it not, you have faith in him. (See Mormon 9:18-27.)

2. When you also repent and watch over your thoughts, you become pure in heart, your inner vessel is cleansed, and you can receive what you ask for. (See Mosiah 4:30.)

3. You are then able to connect your hopes and desires with his power by overcoming all doubts that he can and will help you become single-minded. You then have faith sufficient to perform miracles. (See Moroni 7:20-30 and Mosiah 24:10-17.)

A Mental Foundation for Faith

When you see the word "faith," remember the great meaning it has. Allow a mental window of understanding to open to your inner eye. Here are some of the things you might etch on your memory cells for the word "faith." Each time you read the word "faith," realize that it includes the following:

1. I know Jesus Christ lives!

2. I doubt not that Christ lives and can do all things!

3. Whatever I ask for that is confirmed by the Spirit of Truth is God's will for me and will come to pass! (Keep in mind that it is never God's will to usurp anyone's free agency or to force them to change. It *is* his will that we ask for increased inspiration and spiritual help for our loved ones.) (See Mormon 9:21 and D&C 46:7.)

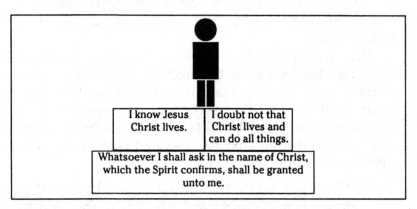

This is the mental foundation you must have to experience miracles in your life. The foundation for your faith consists of those three concepts or belief statements. Picture them as a foundation of granite blocks upon which you must stand to receive the desires of your heart. (See figure above.) To develop this foundation you just need to say (and believe):

1. I have *hope* in Christ, or
2. I *believe* in Christ, or
3. I *know* Christ lives

I have discovered that when people feel that they do not know Christ lives, they are afraid that they cannot use this law. However, you can be at any one of the following levels and still make the law work for you.

King Lamoni had only to express that he *believed* what Ammon was telling him, then he prayed and received a great blessing. (See Alma 18-19.)

You can come to *know* that Jesus Christ lives; *hoping* and *believing* that he lives are the first steps. You will grow in understanding as you ask for light and knowledge on anything you desire to know about; in turn, you will grow in the reality that Christ lives. The ways in which the answers come create more faith. It is an ever-widening and enlarging circle. Faith in Christ begets more understanding and understanding begets more faith and more faith creates miracles in your life, as Jacob describes in Jacob 4:6–8.

Wherefore, we search the prophets, and we have many revelations and the spirit of prophecy; and having all these witnesses we obtain a hope, and our faith becometh unshaken, insomuch that we truly can command in the name of Jesus and the very trees obey us, or the mountains, or the waves of the sea.

Nevertheless, the Lord God showeth us our weaknesses that we may know that it is by his grace, and his great condescensions unto the children of men, that we have power to do these things.

Behold, great and marvelous are the works of the Lord. How unsearchable are the depths of the mysteries of him; and it is impossible that man should find out all his ways. And no man knoweth of his ways save it be revealed unto him; wherefore, brethren, despise not the revelations of God.

In order to use these principles effectively and to keep them in perspective, however, we must remember that:

1. The will of God is not always done in the short-range—only in the eternities. While his purposes are always fulfilled, the Lord allows all men their free agency. They frequently use that agency to break his commandments and to be unkind, thoughtless, and even cruel to others. We may exert all our faith to the accomplishment of a righteous goal and have it rendered impossible in the present moment by the foolish or wicked choices of another person. For instance, we can gain an absolute knowledge that it is the Lord's will that someone else repent. We may fast and pray for years—yet that repentance will never come to pass until the person decides for himself to repent. Therefore, whenever our righteous desire is dependent on any other person, we must recognize that the other person may choose for the rest of his life not to do God's will and that God will not force that

person to do so. Yet, acts done in righteousness are never lost, so our love and efforts for other people will surely bring blessings to our own souls, though not necessarily in the way we expect.

2. Both the timetables and perceptions of time of the Lord are completely different from ours. The Bible tells us that the Lord's thoughts are not our thoughts (Isaiah 55:8). We think in terms of *now*. We think a year is a long time to wait for a righteous desire. But God sees a thousand years as a day. He knows the beginning from the end. We know only yesterday and today. When the Spirit whispers, "Yes, my child, it is my will that you have this blessing," he may mean in the Millennium or after; we, however, assume he means tomorrow or the next day. All these differences in perception may try our faith. But only after the trial of our faith come the blessings.

Developing trust in the Lord is our basic goal. Whether his answer to our prayers is "yes," "no," or "not yet," we must trust that the answer will be for our best good. "All things work together for good to him that loves the Lord." So the process described in this book for applying faith is not a never-fail, cut-and-dried formula. It is not the intent of the author to suggest that it is a way to quickly get all the things you want in life and to have things turn out the way you want them to. The steps for applying faith discussed here are a model—a suggested pattern to experiment with and to use as an exercise in faith in order to make it more real and powerful in your life. Just as we must exercise our muscles to achieve physical fitness, we also need to exercise our faith to achieve spiritual fitness. That means practice and learning through trial and error.

How Does Faith Work?

Since our desire is to learn the laws of faith in order to put them to work in our lives, let us now unpuzzle how faith works.

You know from the scriptures that all men are spirit intelligences. (Abraham 3:22.) You also know that intelligences think and that thinking is your inner self-talk. To think takes mental effort and faith works by your mental effort. In *Lectures on Faith*, page 61, #3, Joseph Smith explains how you work by faith.

> Let us here offer some explanation in relation to faith, that our meaning may be clearly comprehended. We ask, then, what are we to understand by a man's working by faith? We answer—we understand that when a man works by faith he works by mental exertion instead of physical force. It is by words, instead of exerting his physical powers, with which every being works when he works by faith.

How Miracles Will Come

In his book, *Already to Harvest*, Elder Hartman Rector, Jr. tells us that "thoughts produce an effect as literal as physical exertion" (p. 44). It is always by thought and mental exertion first that we bring forth any creation or answers to prayers. The Lord created the world and everything in it in his thoughts before he created it physically. The experience of Alma and the followers of Christ, recorded in Mosiah 24:10-17, tells us how they were delivered because the Lord heard the prayer in their hearts (their thoughts). Their prayers were not ever verbal yet they were powerfully effective. In our thoughts we spiritually create our lives.

Faith Begins with Your Thoughts

If faith works by mental effort, and the tools used are thoughts, then let us learn more about where thoughts come from. To begin, let me share an idea from the book *Life After Life* by Dr. Raymond Moody. The following is an account of a woman who died on the operating table, and then returned to life.

> I was more conscious of my mind at the time than of that physical body. The mind was the most important part, instead of the shape of the body. And before, all my life, it had been exactly reversed. The body was my main interest and what was going on in my mind, well, it was just going on, and that's all. But after this happened, my mind was the main point of attraction, and the body was second—it was only something to encase my mind. (*Life After Life*, p. 91.)

This woman realized that her thoughts stayed with her when she was away from her body. She was still alive, thinking!

Here is the record of an experience taken from the book *Return From Tomorrow* by Dr. George Ritchie. This is Dr. Ritchie's own experience. When he realized he had lost his solidness, his body, so that mortals were not aware of his presence and could not respond to him, he thought, "Am I dead?" Then he said: "But I wasn't dead! How could I be dead and still be awake? Thinking. Experiencing. Death was different. Death was . . . I didn't know. Blanking out. Nothingness. [But] I was me, wide awake, only without a physical body to function in." (pp. 47-48.)

Dr. Ritchie realized he was dead, yet he was still able to think. This same type of experience has been reported by hundreds of people. According to Dr. Moody's newest book, *The Light Beyond*, a 1982 Gallop Poll showed that eight million Americans have had an NDE (Near Death Experience) (p. 16). That is one in twenty adults!

The following story again reveals to us the reality of our spirit/intelligence self. This incident happened in the lives of Bishop and Sister John H. Wells, a former member of the Presiding Bishopric and his wife. It illustrates how we may receive communication from those who have passed on.

Bishop and Sister Wells had a son who was killed in a railroad accident in Emigration Canyon, east of Salt Lake City, Utah. He had been run over by a freight car. Sister Wells received no comfort from the funeral, and she mourned unceasingly for her son.

One day soon after the funeral, as Sister Wells was lying on her bed in a state of great sorrow, her son appeared to her. He told her "Mother, don't mourn. Don't cry. I am all right." Then he told her how the accident had occurred. He also told her that he had tried to make contact with his father as soon as he realized he was in another sphere. He had been unable to do so, however, because his father had been so occupied (in his thoughts) with the affairs of his work. The young man then said, "Tell Father all is well with me, and I don't want you to mourn anymore." (*Come unto Christ,* Ezra Taft Benson, p.18)

These experiences teach that if you were to die right now, you would realize immediately that you are not your body or your brain. You are a spirit intelligence living inside of a body (the Lord's word is temple) which can be influenced for good or evil because both good and evil come into your mind as thoughts.

Now let us go one step further by learning more about the brain and how it works with the "thoughts" you create with your "thinking intelligence."

Understanding the Brain and How It Works

Your brain is not your intelligence; it is merely a servo-mechanism given to you by your Heavenly Father to help you think and act. You might liken the brain to a computer; it does the processing, sorting, and filing of the thoughts and information which you give it. It is a highly sophisticated computer which operates at your command. The conscious mind accepts what you give it and does the recording of the information; the subconscious sorts, files, and stores that material.

The existence of the subconscious mind is an accepted medical fact. All your thoughts and actions actually program the subconscious mind. The data is placed in your mind's storage bank which, according to the Neuropsychology of Achievement, tape # 1 by Syber Vision, contains over 200 billion brain cells.

President John Taylor shares this insight about man being a self-registering machine.

If I had time to enter into this subject alone, I could show you upon scientific principles that man himself is a self-registering machine, his eyes, his ears, his nose, the touch, the taste, and all the various senses of the body, are so many media whereby man lays up for himself a record which perhaps nobody else is acquainted with but himself and when the time comes for the record to be unfolded, all men that have eyes to see, and ears to hear, will be able to read all things as God himself reads them and comprehends

them, and all things, we are told, are naked and open before him with whom we have to do. (See Journal of
Discourses, 26:31 pp.13-14.)

We learn from Syber Vision about the workings of the
brain in relation to learning and achievement. Though we
do not see each other's thoughts, in reality, they do exist.
They are composed of electromagnetic wave forms which
possess energy and matter.

This concept is intriguing. Thought is matter! What implications does this hold for you? According to the laws
of quantum physics, your visual images, which are created
by your thoughts, are also matter which means that any
clear image (of yourself or a situation) you visualize in
your thoughts is translated by your nervous system the
same as if it were real. Thus, if you daily imagine yourself
and your life the way you would like it to be, those
thoughts become the blueprint for your brain and your
nervous system to create the person or life you visualize!

The down side of these facts is that negative thoughts
likewise attract in the same way. The brain does not care
what thoughts it receives because it is a servant, and you
are the master and programmer. If you think more negative thoughts than positive ones, you are programming
yourself an unhappy life.

How Does the Brain Operate?

Since the brain is a servo-mechanism, you need to understand how it operates in order to make the best use
of it. When you understand the brain and how to prop-
erly program it, you are in a good position to be in control of your spirit intelligence, to be master of this
temple we call the body, and to overcome satanic influences. The three figures on the following page will help
give a much clearer understanding of how the brain functions and how the conscious and subconscious mind operate. Figure 1 shows a sketch of the brain shape and
shows how the eye is connected directly to the brain
stem as a living camera—your personal video camera.

Figure 1. The eye is connected directly to the human brain and acts as a camera lens to record what you see; it is your video camera. We all have photographic memory capacity.

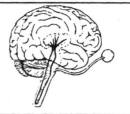

Figure 2. When you are in the alpha state, your mind most readily accepts self-talk (internal, life-directing thoughts)

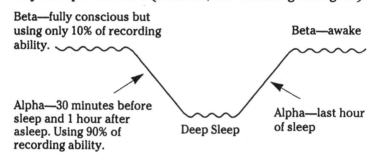

Beta—fully conscious but using only 10% of recording ability.

Beta—awake

Alpha—30 minutes before sleep and 1 hour after asleep. Using 90% of recording ability.

Deep Sleep

Alpha—last hour of sleep

Figure 3. Beta and alpha brain wave patterns.

Beta is a fast moving brain wave that allows only 10% of your recording power to function.

Alpha is a slower moving brain wave that allows 90% of your recording power to function.

Figure 2 shows sleeping and waking brain wave patterns. Figure 3 illustrates the Beta and Alpha brain wave pattern concept.

What Is the Difference Between the Beta and Alpha Levels of the Brain?

At the Beta Level, you are awake and alert. It would be more logical if most of our learning occurred at this level. Yet, interestingly enough, most learning occurs at the

Alpha or relaxed level. What significance does this have as far as your learning and use of time are concerned? Your brain is on record when in Alpha, with 90 percent of power available for you to use. You are in Alpha when you are relaxed as you study, think or meditate, ponder, and pray. You are also there twenty minutes before sleep and during the first hour and the last hour of sleep. When you are in the Alpha brain wave state, your subconscious mind most readily accepts your self-talk as internal life-directing instruction. To easily reach the Alpha level, you can do a deep breathing exercise by inhaling and slowly counting 1-2-3, Hold 1-2-3, Exhale 1-2-3. Repeat five times.

You can choose to take advantage of the Alpha state by recognizing the value of thinking and meditating time and by taking the last thirty minutes before sleep for reprogramming yourself with affirmations, prayer, positive study, and positive self-talk.

Another valuable use of the fact that thoughts, being electrical impulses, flow to the brain and affect the nervous system is the development of a system of pain control called Biofeedback which many doctors now teach their patients. Doctors teach cancer patients, for example, how to mentally visualize an attacking force like, "Pac-Man" images, to "eat up" the cancer cells. The reports show that when a patient does this, the body's ability to fight the malignancy increases noticeably. The patient learns how to control his inner self-talk to communicate with the body at the brain's Alpha level. The patient learns to think instructive thoughts when he is in the relaxed Alpha state. The patient, instead of the pain, then takes charge of his own body.

In their book *Fit For Life*, Harvey and Marilyn Diamond explain that we can also talk to the intelligence in the cells of our body.

Every cell in your body is teeming with life and possesses its own intelligence. Each cell is like a soldier in the army, awaiting its instructions. We are constantly sending messages or commands to our cells, and those commands are carried out diligently. What I'm suggesting is that we can consciously direct our cells to do what we want them to do. The body will bring about whatever result the conscious mind desires. The mind is consciously assessing the body's condition and forming images in line with what it believes to be true. We can literally change our bodies by changing the way we think about them, even in the face of data or evidence that conflicts. (pp. 2-3.)

Alpha-level programming works in the same way. When you learn to relax your body so that the brain waves can shift into Alpha, giving you maximum power, you are in the most productive state to program your brain computer.

Your persistent thoughts create an electromagnetic force which begins an attraction to anything that would help bring into reality the substance of those thoughts. You create your future by what you think about today. You first create your tomorrows spiritually (through your thoughts) before they are created physically.

Using this principle, I suggest that you prepare a self-made recording of an affirmation you wish to program into your subconscious. Then listen to the goal or righteous desire (as it is called in the scriptures) for twenty-one days in a row while you are in this relaxed state giving your brain instructions.

Like Attracts Like

You attract what you continually think about, as James 3:12 points out. He asks, "Can the fig tree . . . bear olive berries?" Those experiences which come into our lives are in kind to that which we have been thinking. "We are like human magnets," Elder Sterling W. Sill believes. "Our deeds, our attitudes, and even our thoughts attract in kind. Like begets like." (*The Laws of Success*, Chapter 7.)

You program the brain by the thoughts you think and the experiences you have. When you lie down to rest, you can program an affirmation to go into your subconscious mind and to be accepted by your brain-servant, to become part of you. Pray for more light and knowledge on this topic to open your mind to understanding.

To have the whole picture and strengthen the whole person—body, mind, and spirit—you can fit the pieces together and program positive perspectives into your brain. By talking back to your thoughts, you can erase negative thoughts and replace them with positive thoughts.

By programming new thoughts, such as persistence or forgiveness, into your brain-servant, you can alter your self-image and thereby alter your life. Thought is live electrical energy and matter which you can create by your own mental effort. You can create faith by your positive inner self-talk, brought forth by your spirit intelligence. It is helpful to repeat to yourself the following: "My spirit intelligence is the real me." Now, ask for more light and knowledge on this topic.

This knowledge about the brain and body has been a missing link—one not fully understood until this era—which can help you learn how to let your spirit intelligence be in control of your body. The brain operates as a computer at your command. Thoughts control the flesh, you control the thoughts, and by controlling your thoughts you become the master over your body.

President Brigham Young said, "The greatest mystery a man ever learned is to know how to control the human mind and bring every faculty and power of the same in subjection to Jesus Christ; this is the greatest mystery we have to learn while in these tabernacles of clay" (*Journal of Discourses* 1:46.) It is also the knowledge we need to be able to effectively use our free agency to chose to live our lives by faith.

Chapter Two

LET US PROVE
THEM HEREWITH:
Moral AGENCY AND HOW
IT APPLIES TO FAITH

A COMMONLY ASKED QUESTION IS: "WHY DO MORE NEGATIVE thoughts come into my mind than positive thoughts?" The answer includes the plan of salvation and why we are here. We can fit these doctrines together. The more pieces of the puzzle we can fit together, the more understandable the picture becomes. The chart on page 21 depicts where we came from and why we are on the earth. I hope this picture will answer the above question for you as it has for me.

In the spirit world we were given our moral agency to choose for ourselves how we would use our lives. There was a great battle in heaven over this issue. Revelation 12:7-9 explains this war:

> And there was war in heaven: Michael and his angels fought against the dragon; and the dragon fought and his angels,
> And prevailed not; neither was their place found any more in heaven.
> And the great dragon was cast out, that old serpent, called the Devil, and Satan, which deceiveth the whole world: he was cast out into the earth, and his angels were cast out with him.

Modern revelation tells us that this war was being fought over our free agency, the basic gift we needed in order to have the opportunity to eventually become like our Heavenly Father and Mother. Satan came before God demanding that he be given all power and he would see that all mankind was saved. The chart and scriptures on

Pre-Earth Existence
Our First Estate

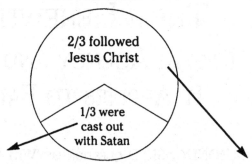

2/3 followed Jesus Christ

1/3 were cast out with Satan

We learn from scriptures that Satan and his angels

1. Will never receive bodies.
2. Want to make us miserable like unto themselves.
3. Want us to hate what we came to get— our bodies.
   (To accomplish this end, Satan tempts people to use profanity and vulgarity to refer to body parts, body functions, and the process by which we create our families.)
4. Want to stop spirits from receiving bodies (abortion).
5. Can speak to our minds and harden our hearts.

In the Pre-Earth Existence, we were

1. Spirit children of God
2. Tutored in many things.
3. Learning the theory of an earth life.
4. Told we would be given a body and become resurrected like Jesus Christ.
5. Told we would be tested on earth to see if we would choose to follow light or darkness.
6. So excited to come to earth that we "shouted for joy."

Earth Life

Earth life
Our Second
Estate

As part of this earth life, we

1. Receive a body.
2. Live by faith and experience a "living laboratory."
3. Learn to listen to the Holy Ghost as we make choices to keep the commandments.
4. Seek to become pure in heart, thoughts, emotions, and actions.

page 22 illustrate this struggle and the choice concerning free agency which we made in the pre-existence. It also shows the communication we are consistently receiving from God and Satan.

Brigham Young taught that because evil spirits will never have their own house (body to live in), they are trying to get into our dwellings. This is one reason we have so much opposition here on earth. (*Journal of Discourses*, II , p. 129.) Brigham Young also taught that:

If men and women understood perfectly their position before God, angels, and men, the place they occupy, and the sphere they act in, they would know they are as independent in their organization as the angels, or as the Gods. (*Journal of Discourses* Vol. II, p. 130.)

In the *Ensign*, July 1984, p. 31, Lawrence R. Peterson, Jr. says the following about the forces we struggle with:

Each of these forces, being spiritual, works directly on the mind of man—or the heart as the scriptures call it—until the individual willfully chooses to obey one and ignore the other. Then the balance of power shifts, and the person begins to move upward to eternal life or downward to destruction and misery. A person who has elected baptism and received the gift of the Holy Ghost has shifted the balance greatly in favor of God's influence, whereas a person whose wickedness has caused his conscience to be "seared with a hot iron," as Paul says in 1 Timothy 4:2, may have put himself wholly within the realm of Satan's influence. The Spirit of the Lord may cease to strive with such a person.

You were given this moral free agency and instructed to prove all things and hold fast to that which is good. You were also instructed to pray always and to seek for knowledge, that you might be given promptings as to what is right for you. In order to do this you must be willing to open your mind and heart, listen to the promptings of the Spirit, and follow them.

This mortal life is the time you were given to study and choose which course you will pursue. A number of scriptures discuss this choice wherein you are to prove all things for yourself. But the Lord has given you to understand that you are also being proved in this life. Abraham 3:25 is perhaps one of the best known quotations on the subject. "And we will prove them herewith, to see if they will do all things whatsoever the Lord their God shall command them."

Too many men and women are acting like robots in these latter days. They are allowing themselves to react to the thoughts which are placed in their minds by the adversary (many times through the media), rather than taking charge of their thoughts and actions and proving that they are willing to follow the Lord's commandments. You must first realize that both good and evil spirits can speak to your spirit. You receive the communication as thoughts or ideas in your mind (most often in your own tone of voice).

The Spoiler initiates negative, doubting, evil, unjustified, fearful, or judgmental thoughts. He also tells you negative thoughts about your weaknesses to make you doubt and fear so that you might be miserable, even as he is miserable. Alma gives us a clear insight in Alma 3:26.

> And in one year were thousands and tens of thousands of souls sent to the eternal world, that they might reap their rewards according to their works, whether they were good or whether they were bad, to reap eternal happiness or eternal misery, according to the Spirit which they listed to obey, whether it be a good spirit or a bad spirit.

You can learn to use the power of discernment and to rule over the evil spirits on every occasion. This is part of the binding of Satan in preparation for the Millennium.

How Can You Distinguish between the Two "Stations" and Choose the Right One?

We all need to improve our spiritual listening skills to be able to hear the whisperings of the Lord or to discern and rid ourselves of the negative and evil whisperings of Satan and his evil spirits.

If It Is Good, It Comes from God

The fact that God is a God of goodness and truth is borne out in the scriptures. James 1:17 says, "Every good gift and every perfect gift is from above, and cometh down from the Father of lights, with whom is no variableness, neither shadow of turning." In Moroni 7:12 we read, "Wherefore, all things which are good cometh of God; and that which is evil cometh of the devil; for the devil is an enemy unto God, and fighteth against him continually and inviteth and enticeth to sin, and to do that which is evil continually." While Satan can deceive us in many ways, he cannot produce counterfeit peace, hope, joy, or testimony of Christ. All good comes from God.

Let No Man Say, "I Am Tempted of God"

Our Heavenly Father does not tempt anyone with evil. Heavenly Father always works by positive, pure, and enlightening thoughts. Your trials and temptations come into your life through your own or someone else's weaknesses or because you give in to the temptations of Satan. The Evil One tempts you wherever you are weak. James 1:12–14 explains:

> Blessed is the man that endureth temptation: for when he is tried, he shall receive the crown of life, which the Lord hath promised to them that love him.
>
> Let no man say when he is tempted, I am tempted of God: for God cannot be tempted with evil, neither tempteth he any man:
>
> But every man is tempted, when he is drawn away of his own lust [weaknesses], and enticed.

We can learn to feel when a thing is right or feel when it is wrong by tuning in to our emotional responses. I remember at one time in my marriage when I had thoughts come into my mind which were totally foreign to my nature. They went something like this: "Marriage isn't as easy as you thought it would be. You are supposed to be happy when you are married, but you aren't happy. Why don't you just leave? You don't feel the love you felt for your husband when you were first married, so your marriage must be wrong."

I recognized that these thoughts were not my own, and I prayed, "These thoughts are not mine. I need help, Father. I desire for my love to grow, not go."

The Spirit's impressions then told me that in order to destroy a children's home foundation, the Evil One must first destroy the relationship of the parents. That meant my husband and I would be the ones Satan would attack first to get to the children. I remember looking at the pictures of our five children and making a mental decision: "No evil force is going to get these children. The Lord has given us stewardship over them and I will do whatever is necessary to strengthen our marriage to help these five most important people. I love my husband, I love our children, and I will not allow difficulties to be resolved in the ways of the world!" I then asked the Father for the light and knowledge I needed to help me learn to know what I could do to create a happier marriage.

Proverbs 23:7 tells us: "For as he thinketh in his heart, so is he." I learned from the Spirit to watch over my thoughts and to clear all negative impressions which tried to enter there, so that the thoughts I allowed into my mind would express what I truly desired in my marriage and my home. As I did, my marriage and home life began to show the fruits of my change in self-talk. I also called upon the Lord to soften both my heart and my husband's heart that he might also desire to change and so we could each learn to listen more fully to the whisperings of the Spirit to know of each other's needs. I had learned I cannot make anyone change; the natural man (or woman) gets in the way. I needed to ask the Lord to help my husband and I overcome our weaknesses.

What a fascinating experience! Suddenly I realized I was living the laws of faith! I was hoping for things I could not see, praying for light and knowledge, and believing that I would be blessed. A new world opened up to me. I learned that righteous desires really do matter to the Lord and that he is waiting to bless us as we learn to ask for his help and as we overcome any doubt that he lives and will answer our prayers.

Satan Addresses You in Your Mind as "You"

Since you now know that Satan speaks to you in your mind and that you most often hear him in your own tone of voice, you are ready to see that Satan addresses you as "you." When you speak to yourself about yourself, do you think of yourself as "you"? Of course not! You think of yourself and address yourself as "I" and your self-talk is always thought and spoken in that way. "I will do this" or "I like that."

This is one way you can know when the whisperings are from Satan. Learn to listen to your self-talk and discern whether you are hearing "you" or "I" spoken in your mind. When you hear negative messages using the word "you," you can know these whisperings are from the Spoiler, who is seeking to get you to listen to him so he can make you confused, double-minded, critical, or unhappy.

Another way you can know which station you are tuning into is by how you feel about yourself and the world. Do your thoughts leave you feeling good and uplifted? Or do they leave you feeling angry, depressed, or critical? If they are negative and destructive, you can know they are from the Spoiler.

Negative Input from Satan Can Affect Your Faith and Keep You from Receiving Miracles

In order to stop negative thoughts, you must exercise mental effort and faith in Jesus Christ. You do this through erasing negative thoughts and replacing them with positive inner self-talk.

You did not create those thoughts, and you can command them to leave. You can "erase and replace" or say, "I choose to clear these thoughts." Here is a mental exercise which I find totally clears away negative thoughts and feelings. In fact, my life has changed since I have learned this exercise. Begin by getting in touch with what you desire to discard. Then ask yourself the following questions:

1. Would I release this negative thought or feeling if I could? (Answer "yes.")
2. Could I release it by my faith in Jesus Christ to help me? (Answer "yes.")
3. When would I release it and replace it with pure thoughts? (Answer "now.")

Even if you know the thoughts are true, if they are negative, quickly get rid of them and replace them with constructive, uplifting, and positive thoughts. Remember that to erase a negative thought you must first discern that it is negative (even though it may be true!) and then mentally command yourself to clear it. One of the lies Satan tells us is that if something is true, we should focus on it—no matter how negative it is.

Discernment Is a Gift of the Spirit

You can ask for spiritual gifts, such as the gift of discernment, by praying in faith. The Lord tells us in D&C 46:11, "For all have not every gift given unto them; for there are many gifts, and to every man is given a gift by the Spirit of God."

One of the spiritual gifts you need is mentioned in verse 23: "the discerning of spirits." Your ability to fine-tune your perception of the Spirit and to discern the influence of evil spirits is a gift and should be diligently developed as a safeguard against deception.

The Fruits of Faith

In the *Teachings of the Prophet Joseph Smith,* I found this statement:

Because faith is wanting, the fruits are. No man since the world was had faith without having something along with it. The ancients quenched the violence of fire, escaped the edge of the sword, women received their dead, etc. By faith the worlds were made. A man who has none of the gifts has no faith; and he deceives himself, if he supposes he has. (p. 270.)

Erasing Negative Thought Takes Effort

By your mental efforts, you can give your mind commands and dictate your thoughts. Since you have your moral agency you can order the negative, doubting, evil, judgmental thoughts, or unjustified fears (all of which come from Satan) to leave. Then you can think the thoughts you desire and call for angels and a shield of protection from God to help you overcome evil influences.

I have learned to discern if a thought is a positive thought or a negative thought. I do not ask myself whether it is true or false because thoughts can be true and still be negative and destructive. For example, my thought, "My husband and I are so different" is true; men and women do think differently. Perhaps my husband and I think even more differently than most couples. That truth, however, did not mean I was justified in leaving my husband. I have a friend who got a divorce for this reason. Who spoiled that marriage by using a truth in a negative way? The Spoiler is the one who will use any truth in a negative way to destroy anyone who will listen!

Be alert. As soon as you notice a persistent thought knocking on your mental door, ask yourself this question: "Is this thought positive or negative?" If you discern that it is negative, ask yourself these questions: (1) Can I release this thought through my faith in Jesus Christ to help me? (Answer "yes.") (2) When will I let it go? (Answer "now.") Then replace that negative thought with a positive hope or desire. For example, if someone has hurt your feelings and you are thinking negative thoughts about that individual, say "I choose to release these thoughts. By my faith in Jesus Christ, I choose to forgive this person. I seek more light and knowledge on how to better work with people in the future." Now that you have switched your mental station to a positive station, inspiration can come to you from the Lord because you have asked for it.

In James 4:7 we read: "Submit yourselves therefore to God. Resist the devil, and he will flee from you." This principle is a great safeguard against Satan. I take James's advice to resist the devil literally. I resist Satan by not allowing the impure or negative thoughts he would like to plant in my mind to remain there. If I am having trouble clearing my mind, I say "Father, by my faith in Jesus Christ, I ask for the shield of faith and purity to be thickened and for angels to attend me to keep me from having impure thoughts. I know that thy Son liveth, and I doubt him not."

I have been working on recognizing and clearing judgmental thoughts about myself and other people. I am tired of having judgmental thoughts and of acting as if they have a right to be in my mind. No one has called me to be a judge and I do not get paid for my judgments, so I decided to give up the job of judging. When negative, judgmental thoughts come, I say to myself, "I choose to clear these thoughts. I am no judge. The Lord is the judge." I replace judgmental thoughts with this thought: "I lovingly allow others to live their own lives and to' use their free agency to make their own decisions."

James continues his advice in verse 8 by saying: "Draw nigh to God, and he will draw nigh to you. Cleanse your hands, ye sinners; and purify your hearts, ye double minded."

What Does it Mean to Be Double-minded?

Being double-minded means that you have believed some of the negative, doubting, evil, or fearful thoughts Satan has put into your mind. It means that even though you may be a righteous person, you are allowing yourself to be led one step into Satan's territory. You should avoid double-mindedness as if it were a disease because it can stop inspiration and miracles from coming to you. When you are double-minded, you can receive nothing from the Lord because you are not "tuned in" to receive inspiration. Your thoughts and energy cannot go in two different directions at once. When you are listening to Satan, that focus requires all your energy. But when you use your mental energy to get rid of all negative thoughts and to become single-minded, your thoughts and energy will be focused, directed, and powerful.

Changing Life's Negatives into Positives

Positive fruits from the Spirit—the Tree of Life:

—Say, "I believe in Christ." This gives you doubting not faith in Jesus Christ in your heart or thoughts. The fruits of this action are:

   —Inspiration (personal revelation) comes into your thoughts and is positive, pure, and enlightening.

   —Light or love

   —Receiving answers to your prayers

   —Praying for light and knowledge about your concerns

   —Hope, faith, and knowledge

   —Belief

   —A broken (softened) heart

      —Changing thoughts and emotions

      —Opening up to the spiritual radio station of the mind—the instrument of the Spirit

   —Feeling happy, peaceful, and cheerful

   —Being consistent and good-natured in the home and out of the home—being one

   —Being able to say "I'm sorry" when you offend someone. "Inasmuch as ye have done it unto one of the least of these my brethren, ye have done it unto me."

   —Feeling that you love yourself

   —Loving your neighbor as yourself

   —Catching others doing something right and telling them

   —Being single-minded

   —Having positive inner self-talk

   —Forgiving (releasing before you need to do so)

   —Changing a negative thought to a positive one by using the "Would I? Could I? When?" procedure (See page 28.)

Negative fruits from the Spoiler—the Tree of Good and Evil:
- —No control over thoughts
- —Sinspiration in your thoughts
- —Judgmental thoughts of self or others
- —Doubt or wavering thoughts about your desires in prayer
- —Unbelief that God means what he says
- —Feeling fearful emotions
- —Hearts hardened by thoughts and emotions
- —Guilty, unforgiving feelings for self or others
- —Profanity coming into the mind
- —Immoral thoughts knocking on your mental door
- —Having thoughts of leaving your family
- —Being inconsistent: behaving differently in your home compared to out of the home
- —Lying, cheating, stealing, killing, or having thoughts of suicide
- —Negative inner self-talk
- —Thinking that God does not hear your prayers
- —Coveting or wishing for things inappropriately
- —Feeling depressed
- —Being double minded (James 1:2-8)
- —Teasing others about their weaknesses
- —Disliking yourself
- —Thinking about breaking the word of wisdom
- —Believing false traditions of the fathers, such as "I do not need to say 'I'm sorry.' It is not easy for me so I do not have to say it."
- —Being critical

Our Faith Will Be Tried

Ether 12:6 tells us, "Wherefore dispute not because ye see not, for ye receive no witness until after the trial of your faith." This is a principle we will discuss throughout the book.

Ask of God, Nothing Wavering

James 1:2-8, which also discusses how our faith will be tried, uses the term "nothing wavering" to tell us that we must learn to replace the negative, fearful thoughts with positive ones. As familiar as the verses are that Joseph Smith quoted, it is helpful to study them in this context.

> My brethren, count it all joy when ye fall into divers temptations [trials];
>
> Knowing this, that the trying of your faith worketh patience.
>
> But let patience have her perfect work, that ye may be perfect and entire, wanting nothing.
>
> If any of you lack wisdom, let him ask of God, that giveth to all men liberally, and upbraideth not; and it shall be given him.
>
> But let him ask in faith, nothing wavering. For he that wavereth is like a wave of the sea driven with the wind and tossed.
>
> For let not that man think that he shall receive anything of the Lord.

A Double-minded Man Is Unstable in All His Ways.

D&C 4:5 reminds you that you need to keep your "eye single to the glory of God." Are you staying single-minded? What can a single-minded person do? Through your faith in Jesus Christ, you can access the power of God and do all things. Like the people of the City of Enoch who were of one mind and one heart, you can receive the Spirit and power of the Lord and receive the righteous desires of your heart.

Below are two other instances of single-minded faith, as told in the Book of Mormon. The stories of the sons of Mosiah and of Alma the younger and the two thousand stripling warriors are dramatic examples of the power of faith.

Alma and the Sons of Mosiah

Alma the younger and the sons of Mosiah had persecuted members of the church and the people of God, a practice which caused their fathers great sorrow and pain. Yet, through the faith and prayers of Alma, Mosiah, and others, their sons received a dramatic heavenly manifestation: an angel appeared to them and severely chastised them for their wickedness. As a result of this experience, Alma the younger and the sons of Mosiah repented and dedicated the rest of their lives to making restitution for their sins by doing missionary work. Their missionary labors involved great faith and works. Through their faith, they were able to convert King Lamoni and then entire nations of Lamanites.

The Lamanites who were converted at that time covenanted that they would never again go to war with their brethren. The old king said, "Now, my best brethren, since God hath taken away our stains, and our swords have become bright, then let us stain our swords no more with the blood of our brethren . . . as a testimony to our God." (Alma 24:12, 15.)

The 2,000 Stripling Warriors

The Lamanites who remained outside the church sought to take advantage of those who had joined the church. Because the converted Lamanites had covenanted to fight no more, the Nephites were forced to take up arms to defend their brethren. The sons of the Lamanite converts had not taken the oath, and they determined that they would go forth and defend their people from the invaders. Alma 53:18-19 tells us: "Now behold, there were two thousand of those young men, who entered into this covenant and took their weapons of war to defend their country . . . and they would that Helaman should be their leader."

In a later epistle to Moroni, Helaman praised these young men who said, "Behold our God is with us, and he will not suffer that we should fall." (Alma 56:46.) They had been taught by their mothers that if they did not doubt, God would deliver them.

To Helaman's joy, not one of them perished in battle, although they received many wounds. He continues his narrative with this stirring conclusion:

And now, their preservation was astonishing to our whole army, yea, that they should be spared while there was a thousand of our brethren who were slain. And we do justly ascribe it to the miraculous power of God, because of their exceeding faith in that which they had been taught to believe—that there was a just God, and whosoever did not doubt, that they should be preserved by his marvelous power. (Alma 57:26.)

These two thousand young men exercised total faith. They did not doubt that the Lord could preserve them. The Lord blessed them because they were single-minded.

In contrast to this story of faith, the Lord explains in D&C 67:1, 3 what can happen to those who do not control fear and doubt:

Behold and hearken, O ye elders of my church, who have assembled yourselves together, whose prayers I have heard, and whose hearts I know, and whose desires have come up before me.

Ye endeavored to believe that ye should receive the blessing which was offered unto you; but behold, verily I say unto you there were fears in your hearts, and verily this is the reason that ye did not receive.

These men allowed the Spoiler to put doubts in their minds. Their double-mindedness triggered their emotional response of fear, a response which kept them from receiving a promised blessing.

After you exercise faith, you will notice how negative thoughts try to get your attention. Positive thought is the expression of your faith; the presence of negative thought is the trial of that faith. Ether tells us, "Ye receive no witness until after the trial of your faith." (Ether 12:6.) If we can rid ourselves of negative thoughts and keep thinking positive thoughts about our hopes and desires, our faith will bear the fruit of miracles in our lives. This is the proof of faith.

The Mustard Seed

The idea of hoping for something you cannot see is similar to the message given in the parable of the mustard seed. That seed may be so small you can scarcely see it. Though the seed is small, all you must do is plant and nurture it and it will grow. The same is true of your hopes and desires. As you tell the Lord about them and mentally doubt not, they too will take root and grow because you have planted and nourished a righteous desire through your thoughts and faith. Then comes the fruit of faith, which is miracles. You can hope for things you do not see, and extend your positive mental effort, which is connected to your doubting not faith in Jesus Christ. Then when you ask, you will receive your righteous desires. Now is the time to start learning how to improve your life by faith; to have an Enoch experience; and to start receiving what you ask for because of your doubting-not faith in Jesus Christ.

Doubt Not—Fear Not

The lost books of the Bible have a great deal to say about doubting and double-mindedness and their effects in our lives. The following quotes are from 2 Hermes 9:1-11, taken from the Pseudepigrapha, published in 1911.

Remove from Thee All Doubting

Remove from thee all doubting:
And question nothing at all,
when thou asketh anything of the Lord:
Saying within thyself: how shall I be able to
ask anything of the Lord and receive it,
Seeing I have so greatly sinned against him?

Do not think thus, but turn unto the Lord with
all thy heart,
And ask of him without doubting.

Wherefore purify thy heart from
all the vices of this present world;
And thou shalt receive whatsoever good
things thou shalt ask
And nothing shall be wanting unto thee
of all thy petitions:
If thou shalt ask of the Lord without doubting . . .

But they that are not such shall obtain none
of those things which they shall ask,
For they that are full of faith ask all things

with confidence and receive from the Lord
Because they ask without doubting . . .

Wherefore, purify the heart from doubting.
And put on faith, and trust in God,
and thou shalt receive all that thou shalt ask.
But if thou shouldest chance to ask somewhat
and not receive it,
Yet do not therefore doubt, because thou hast
not presently received the petition of thy soul . . .

But do not leave off to ask
and then thou shalt receive . . .
Else if thou shalt cease to ask, thou must complain
of thyself, and not of God.
That he has not given unto thee
what thou didst desire.

Consider therefore this doubting,
how cruel and pernicious it is:
And how it utterly roots out many from the faith,
who were very faithful and firm.
For this doubting is the daughter of the devil,
and deals very wickedly with the servants of God.

Despise it, therefore, and thou shalt rule over
it on every occasion.
Put on a firm and powerful faith;
For faith promises all things and perfects all things.
But doubting will not believe that it shall
obtain anything, by all that it can do.

Faith cometh from above, from God:
and hath great power.
But doubting is an earthly spirit, and
proceedeth from the devil.
And has no strength.

Do thou therefore keep the virtue of faith,
And depart from doubting in which is no virtue
And thou shalt live unto God.

(*The Lost Books of the Bible*, Cleveland: World
Publishing Company, 1926, pp. 221-22.)

Doubt and unbelief keep you from receiving miracles.
Unbelief, hardness of heart, and double-mindedness are

the things with which the Lord is displeased for they can restrain him from showering us with needed miracles.

The scriptures express this idea in many places. For example, 1 Nephi 15:11 says that "If ye will not harden your hearts, and ask me in faith, believing that ye shall receive, . . . surely these things shall be made known unto you." Matthew 13:58 also supports this idea: "And he did not many mighty works there because of their unbelief."

A third example is Ether 4:15:

> Behold, when ye shall rend that veil of unbelief which doth cause you to remain in your awful state of wickedness, and hardness of heart, and blindness of mind, then shall the great and marvelous things which have been hid up from the foundation of the world from you—yea, when ye shall call upon the Father in my name, with a broken heart and a contrite spirit, then shall ye know that the Father hath remembered the covenant which he made unto your fathers, O house of Israel.

Overcoming Fears

The following letter tells of an experience of a sister who discovered what she could do to overcome some spiritually dangerous fears.

> Like many, we set a goal to go to the temple each month. It was a two-hour trip each way, which meant that we were gone from home at least six hours. We had five young children and I hated to leave them that long. Not because they would be unhappy or sad, or because I didn't trust those I left them with, but because I knew that Satan is real and I was afraid of what he might "engineer" while I was gone. In the months after we set this goal, I began to listen to the wrong thoughts and let fear grow strong in my heart. Each month grew to be a greater and greater struggle for me to leave my precious little ones and go to the temple. I prayed and tried to have faith so that I could have peace, but the struggle continued.

> In the late spring, my husband and I attended your lecture on faith from which I learned that all the bad thoughts I had been having were not my own. I was free to decide which voice I would listen to and which thoughts would be mine.

I began to pray constantly for a feeling of peace concerning our trips to the temple. On the days we would be planning to attend the temple, I would think about it all day, and I would try to replace each negative thought with a good one. I also made a greater effort to read my scriptures every day. I tried in earnest to use my faith to obtain the feeling of peace that I sincerely desired.

However, even with all my efforts, the next month it was all I could do to get myself out the door. I felt more afraid than ever before. I told my husband I didn't understand why it was so hard for me. I wanted desperately to stay home with my children, and yet I felt a real sense of the importance of going.

As the session began, it was as if I couldn't keep up with my thoughts. I was learning all kinds of things, things about my Church calling as Primary President, and about my husband and children and their needs. Then I heard a voice say, "Julie." I turned to find my sister Marie, who had died as an infant when I was only eight years old. I don't know how I knew who she was, but I remember being surprised at how much like my younger sister Jane she was.

She was beautiful. She was standing in the aisle, her feet not touching the ground. She was smiling and I knew immediately that she loved me. I thought, "You're not dead! You're alive! You're not a stiff little baby buried up in Idaho!" I was given to know that she was a celestial being. We spoke to each other but not as mortals speak. It was through our minds—our thoughts. She said, "It's very important for you to come to the temple every month. And you don't have to worry anymore because I will watch over your children for you." She smiled again and was gone, and I knew where she went: to my house to watch over my little ones.

I was filled with joy and gratitude. I was overwhelmed with the kindness of our Father. And I was filled with peace.

After the session, in the dressing room, I was pondering what had happened when I again felt Marie's presence. She said, "Please tell Mom and Dad that I love them."

What a wonderful experience to gain not only peace about leaving my little ones while I attended the temple, but also to receive a heavenly visitation from my sister—a sister who was not sleeping in the grave but who was very much alive and ready and willing to help me! How great are the gifts of our God!

I marvel that this experience happened to me. I testify that it happened on 23 June 1988 in the Arizona Temple. I have since come upon this scripture: 2 Timothy 1:7-9 "For God hath not given us the spirit of fear; but of power, and of love, and of a sound mind."

Julie Burk, Globe, Arizona

Fear is an insidious form of double-mindedness. The forces of evil only need to whisper or send something into your mind to trigger an emotion of fear which can in turn cause doubting and double-mindedness. The prophet Job was sorely tested in this way. He said, "For the thing which I greatly feared is come upon me, and that which I was afraid of is come unto me." (Job 3:25.)

Could it be that the fear placed in Job's mind by Satan allowed him to have more trials than he would have had otherwise? Apparently, fear is one of the tools Satan uses to create weaknesses in otherwise strong and faithful people.

Being Double-minded

You are double-minded if you give place in your mind to both spiritual radio-like stations. Matthew 6:24 expresses it like this: "No man can serve two masters: for either he will hate the one, and love the other; or else he will hold to the one, and despise the other."

You are double-minded when you:

1. Feel unjustified and prolonged fear in your life without making efforts to overcome it.
2. Feel depressed for allowing negative thoughts to stay in your mind.
3. Contribute to contention with your spouse or family members.
4. Are offended too easily.
5. Do not communicate well with family members or companions.
6. Have prolonged feelings of self-dislike or self-criticism.
7. Lose the desire to grow, to improve, and to serve.

8. Stop caring about others.

9. Do not hold personal prayers in order to receive inspiration from the Lord.

10. Allow doubtful thoughts to take over your mind—thoughts concerning the righteous desires of your heart which have been confirmed by the Spirit, but not yet received.

A person who is double-minded has thoughts which are tattered, negative, and weak. What does it take to stop negative, doubting, evil, or fearful thoughts? It takes your positive mental effort connected to your faith in Jesus Christ. How do you use positive mental effort to make faith work for you? You command your own thoughts. Through your mental effort, you control the thoughts you allow to stay in your mind. Because your faith is tried constantly while you are here on the earth, you need to be on guard daily.

To be able to receive the blessings and miracles you desire, you can learn to quickly release all negative attitudes and replace them with positive hopes and desires. Always remember that:

• Erasing a negative thought takes your mental effort which is your faith at work.

• When doubts or fears enter your mind, again, use your inner self-talk to mentally ask yourself, (1) Would I release this negative thought or feeling if I could? (Answer "yes.") (2) Could I release it by my faith in Jesus Christ to help me? (Answer "yes.") (3) When would I let it go? (Answer "now.")

• Use the above technique whenever negative or evil thoughts invade your mind. After you have released the negative or evil thoughts, replace them with positive, pure thoughts. Then express your thanks. This is expressed in the scripture, "Get thee behind me, Satan." (Matthew 16:23.)

The words of the song "I Have A Garden" (p. G-18 of the new *Primary Song Book*) express this concept well. The following is verse two:

I have a garden, a secret garden
Where thoughts like flowers grow day by day;
'Tis I must choose them, and tend and use them
And cast all wrong ones like weeds away.
Goodness and love are seeds that I sow;
God up above will help me I know,
To keep my garden, my heart's own garden,
A place where beauty will always grow.

You Are a Mental Gardener!

You plant seeds of thought daily in your life. If in your backyard garden:

1. You plant peas, what will you get?
2. You plant corn, what will you get?
3. You plant beans, what will you get?

According to the law of the harvest, you will reap only what you sow. Galatians 6:7 tells us, "Be not deceived; God is not mocked: for whatsoever a man soweth, that shall he also reap." If you plant one kernel of corn, will you get only one kernel back? No. You receive an abundance. The law of abundance applies to your thoughts as well.

As a mental gardener in life, you will grow negative attitudes if you plant thoughts such as:

1. I have no friends.
2. I am dumb.
3. I am fat.
4. I am ugly.
5. I have an unhappy marriage.
6. I am not a good parent.
7. I hate life.

You and I are literally planting seeds of thought every moment of our lives. Because of the law of the harvest and the law of abundance, the seeds of thought we plant can only give us back an increase of their own kind in abundance. If our thoughts are negative, then we will find that our harvest is the opposite of what we want. Negative thoughts attract negative experiences and positive thoughts attract positive experiences. Which kind of experiences do you want?

How Satan Uses Entertainment to Influence Us

Wavering, negative, or fearful thoughts about your hopes and desires cannot come from the Lord but only from Satan. I have come to realize that Satan uses his knowledge of how we think and process information to influence us negatively. Dr. Dean Black of the BioResearch Foundation says that we are what is called an "open system." This, he explains, means that everything we see or hear is transferred to our mental system and influences us. Satan is successful in promoting immorality and evil through movies and television because of this transference. He knows that one of the best and most effective ways to negatively influence a whole nation is through its entertainment.

As the level of public entertainment falls, the level of our private morals will fall as well unless we are aware of possible pitfalls and are very careful to avoid entertainment which could influence us negatively. Satan is successfully programming a whole nation to accept a gradually deteriorating moral standard.

Benjamin Franklin said that "Only a virtuous people are capable of freedom. As nations become corrupt and vicious, they have more need of masters." If this is true, it is easy to see that the United States of America is in grave danger. Many nations have been destroyed through immorality, a sin Satan and our enemies are using as America's Trojan horse. Our only hope is to repent and become pure in heart.

Repentance and Forgiveness

Repentance and forgiveness are the methods by which we can achieve single-mindedness. They are, therefore, important in fulfilling the laws of faith and in achieving joy. You can learn how to repent and to forgive when you ask, seek, and knock.

To Him Who Repents

Yea, he that repenteth and exerciseth faith, and bringeth forth good works, and prayeth continually without ceasing—unto such it is given to know the mysteries of God; yea, unto such it shall be given to reveal things which never have been revealed; yea, and it shall be given unto such to bring thousands of souls to repentance, even as it has been given unto us to bring these our brethren to repentance. (Alma 26:22.)

As you become aware of your mistakes, you will take the steps required to obtain full repentance. You must first recognize your wrongdoing and feel sorrow for it. You must then make a confession to the Lord, to the person whom you have wronged, and, when needed, to the bishop. You must also offer the person wronged any possible restitution. Finally, you need to forgive yourself of each mistake. Until you can forgive yourself, you will not be able to love yourself completely. If you are not able to forgive and love yourself, how will you be able to love others? The Lord has taught us that "Thou shalt love thy neighbor as thyself." (D&C 59:6.) It is literally true that you can only love your neighbor as you learn to love yourself. The closer you get to the Lord and feel his love for you, the easier that commandment becomes.

You are often harder on yourself than you are on anyone else. Satan likes to continually remind you of little mistakes you have made. Unhealthy guilt occurs when you rehash and relive those memories, as Satan wants you to. This kind of guilt negates real repentance and forgiveness and allows the Evil One to mentally attack you again and again.

As you forgive yourself, you will be able to erase the memory of any pain from the mental storage banks of your subconscious mind. You will remember the situations that caused the pain, but instead of reliving the pain you felt, you will learn from the memory to avoid making similar mistakes in the future.

When you are in the process of repenting, you may be tempted and fall again. Even in this situation, the Lord has said that you can ask for his forgiveness and help. When you call upon the Lord for his help, you will have this added strength to avoid repeating your mistake. You can never be cleansed until you have learned to repent and to forgive yourself and others. The next exercise will help you learn to forgive. It will teach you to erase the mistakes, wrongdoings, or wrong thoughts of which you have been guilty and to replace them with positive, pure, and enlightening thoughts and actions.

Adapt the "Erase and Replace—I Forgive" script to your situation then read it to yourself each night just before bed; or make a tape of it and play the tape just as you retire. Play it faithfully each night for the next twenty-one nights. When a negative situation arises later, you can read the script or play the tape again and release the negative emotions caused by the situation. Also, enjoy using the "Could I? Would I? When?" procedure, found on page 28.

Do not be too disturbed if you find yourself dropping off to sleep in the middle of your tape. Your subconscious is still learning, recording, and storing this self-talk. In the Alpha level, your memory is set on "record" so your brain will be busy clearing away the guilt and fear which you have harbored.

You will find as you continue to use this method that you are feeling more cheerful and less subject to depression, moodiness, and fear. You are actually fortifying yourself against the onslaught of the Spoiler. You are putting yourself in charge, rather than allowing him to be in control. What a good, strengthening experience this can be! As your inner self is cleansed, you can more easily discern and listen to the positive, pure, and enlightening still, small voice of the Spirit.

Erase and Replace Script

Instructions: Adapt the wording of the script to apply to you so that the wording feels perfectly comfortable to you. Then read your own positive affirmations aloud each night for twenty-one nights while sitting or lying in a relaxed position. Read very slowly. You may also record this program on a tape and play it just before you go to sleep at night. After twenty-one days, the program can be reaffirmed simply by saying, "I erase and replace." The following is an example of an erase and replace script.

I feel relaxed . . . so relaxed . . . as I slowly drift into a most satisfying state of relaxation. All mental or physical tension is now released. I erase it. As it dissipates, I feel the warmth of my body as my blood flows, freely circulating and bringing health. Daily relaxation is good for me. As I rest, I now erase from my memory's storage banks every unhappy experience of my past, the feelings of sorrow connected to them, and even all negative reactions connected to them. I happily and easily let them go. I release and clear myself. I am grateful for every experience I have had. I know that each experience is a stepping stone to greater knowledge; even negative experiences can be used for my good.

I now forgive myself for every mistake I have ever made. I realize that when I am guilty of making a mistake, I can follow the Lord's law of repentance . . . that of recognition, sorrow, confession, restitution, and asking for forgiveness.

I know that out of each experience in life, some good must surely come to me. I grow stronger with each experience. I am strong with the Lord by my side. With his help, I am stronger than any problem life brings to me. The full application of the principle of repentance and forgiveness now allows me to forgive myself for every mistake I have ever made. I forgive myself. I forgive anyone who has ever wronged me in any way.

This gospel principle of forgiveness releases me from any negative feelings I have about myself. I love myself. I love my neighbor as myself. I feel the joy of my self-acceptance in my powerful subconscious which gives me the power I need to love others. I accept myself. I accept others as they are. My self-acceptance frees me to be able to change that which must be changed, to grow, and to improve in areas I desire. I am (Create a positive statement of your own to personalize this affirmation.)

I let go of any fears which unjustly rule my life. I love life. This is a happy day. People are a joy to me. I need them and they need me. I am a valuable human being. I am aware of my great worth. There are things to be done by me which are done better by me than by any other person. There is no one who can exactly duplicate my efforts. I am pleased. I love myself. I accept myself completely. I am free . . . free to be me completely within the gospel plan. Now, because I have supplied myself with these priceless qualities and feelings of love, forgiveness, and acceptance, I have them to give. I give them freely. I now feel a sweet, joyful sense of self-love and self-determination filling my life every waking and sleeping hour. My life is a joy to me!

I now enjoy restful sleep and arise when I must, renewed and refreshed. I now release and clear myself. I erase and replace. I trust the Lord to lead my life.

Repentance Is Part of the Perfection Process

Earth life is a very humbling experience. Every day we must deal with negative or evil thoughts. I have learned, however, that the Lord does not require perfection *now*. It is our efforts to repent and have constant control over our thoughts that make us worthy to go to the Lord and ask for the desires of our hearts.

Christ was the only one who ever achieved perfection during mortality. We have been given the ordinance of the sacrament because we are not yet perfect. The Lord, in his mercy, gives us the opportunity to renew our covenants and to be cleansed of our sins each week in order that we may start anew and continue to strive for perfection.

This life, then, is a testing time to help us learn to make righteous decisions. A vital part of this learning process is taking advantage of the repentance process. We can constantly improve our ability to tune in to the spiritual communication the Lord offers us and turn away from Satan's promptings. By doing this, we may be guided by the Spirit, make more and more righteous decisions, and experience many of the miracles we are seeking.

Chapter Three

Understanding How Satan, "The Spoiler," Works

LATTER-DAY REVELATION CONFIRMS THE BIBLICAL TEACHING THAT the devil is a reality and that he strives to lead men and women away from the work of God. One of the major techniques of the devil is to cause human beings to think they are following God's ways, when in reality they are following Satan's path. He is miserable in his situation and he seeks to make us miserable as well.

In Greek, the word "devil" means "slanderer, demon, adversary." In Hebrew, the word devil means "spoiler"; this term describes him well.

The LDS Bible Dictionary, page 656, which offers further information regarding the devil, points out that the devil is an enemy of righteousness and of those who seek to do the will of God. Literally a spirit son of God, he was at one time an angel in authority in the presence of God. However, he rebelled in that premortal life, in opposition to the plan of salvation, championed by Jehovah (Jesus Christ). He also persuaded a third of the spirit children of the Father to rebel with him. "Thus came the devil and his angels." (D&C 29:37.) They were then cast out of heaven and denied the experience of mortal bodies and earth life.

Satan uses a system of thought input similar to the one described in the Introduction. He works by putting negative, doubting, evil, fearful, or judgmental thoughts into our minds. His goal is to spoil our lives and our miracles. Consider some of the things the scriptures have to say about the workings of Satan.

He Whispers in Their Ears

For behold, at that day shall he [the Spoiler] rage [cause to be at war] in the hearts [thoughts and emotions] of the children of men, and stir them up to anger against that which is good.

And behold, others he flattereth away, and telleth them there is no hell; and he saith unto them: I am no devil, for there is none—and thus he whispereth in their ears. (2 Nephi 28:20, 22.)

Lying Sent Forth by Satan to Harden Their Hearts

And it came to pass that from this time forth there began to be lyings sent forth among the people, by Satan, to harden their hearts, to the intent that they might not believe in those signs and wonders which they had seen; but notwithstanding these lyings and deceivings the more part of the people did believe, and were converted unto the Lord." (3 Nephi 1:22.)

Satan Hath Put It into Their Hearts

And, behold, Satan hath put it into their hearts to alter the words which you have caused to be written, or which you have translated, which have gone out of your hands.

For he hath put into their hearts to do this, that by lying they may say they have caught you in the words which you have pretended to translate.

For behold, he has put it into their hearts to get thee to tempt the Lord thy God, in asking to translate it over again." (D&C 10:10, 13, 15.)

How Does the Spoiler Work to Spoil Your Life?

As we have said, you are like a live receiving set attuned to spiritual communications sent from beings you cannot see; there are two distinct stations from which to receive communications. The voice of good and the voice of evil are around you all the time.

D&C 29:39 explains the reason for this: "And it must needs be that the devil should tempt the children of men, or they could not be agents unto themselves; for if they never should have bitter they could not know the sweet."

Because of your moral agency you have the choice of whether you will tune in to the positive station, which gives light and knowledge, or open up the negative airways. Interestingly, you need to ask for information in order to open up the positive airways; whereas, the opposite station needs no invitation at all. "Sinspiration" is always there. Satan's voice may be very subtle and very cunning. The voice of doubt, fear, anger, envy, pride, and greed are all the voices of Satan; you must learn to recognize them as such. If you are aware of who, what, and where Satan is, then you will be more able to build up your armor of protection to withstand his fiery darts. Satan's most potent weapon is negative thoughts. He may put into your mind negative thoughts about yourself: "You can't find a better job, so why try?" or "You're ugly. No one wants you." He can also make you think negative thoughts about others or place in your mind prejudiced thoughts about people who are not of your race. He can even project an immoral thought into your mind and then drag you down further by accusing you of being the creator of the thought. He sends the impressions out to you, then he says: "Look what you're thinking. What makes you think you are such a good Latter-day Saint/Christian? If your friends knew what you are thinking, they wouldn't want to be your friends."

In this way, he whispers in your ear to make you react through the body's emotions. You may mentally judge yourself because of the thoughts he puts into your mind and feel depressed, angry, fearful, or guilty. You judge yourself to be evil, when, in fact, you should discern that negative or immoral thoughts come from him. You have the option to sweep these thoughts from your mind. Unless you take immediate, firm action to root out negative thoughts and command them to leave, you may end up believing them. Satan does his work well. If we believe his lies at hurtful times in our lives and accept them as our own thoughts, we store sorrow, pain, and guilt in our body tissues to be retrieved and used against us in the future.

By mental effort, you can give your mind commands and choose which thoughts you allow to remain in your mind. When you choose to tune in to the Lord's positive station, the "light" is on and you can see your direction. When you listen to Satan's channel, the way is dark and you cannot see your pathway. When you do get tuned into the wrong channel, recognize the source of your thoughts and then walk through the three-step system described on page 28.

Trials in the Form of Immoral and Evil Thoughts

As our young family grew and I was learning to be a happy mother, I had an experience which helped me understand the reality of Satan. I went through three months of constant bombardment of evil thoughts which haunted me. "Where were these thoughts coming from?" I wondered; I knew they were not mine. Yet they came to me in my own voice as though they were my own creation. When these immoral thoughts would descend upon me, other thoughts would taunt me, telling me I was a hypocrite. I would say to myself: "No, I will not have these filthy thoughts. They are not mine!"

I had been taught the truth of who I was by the pure example of my parents, Don and Eileen Pearce. While I was a teenager I also had the sweet experience of our stake MIA girl's camp. Good parents and girl's camp, which included the pinecone ceremony (something I used to rid myself of bad habits), were the two most important elements that shaped my character during my youth.

Even though I had developed through these experiences, a deep, abiding testimony and conviction that I would live a clean life, full of service, here I was, years later, in deep despair. I prayed for release from these impure thoughts. Then a wonderful thing happened: a new neighbor told me an experience that held the key to my release.

As my new neighbor, JoAnn Boyd, and I became acquainted, I learned that she had been a missionary in my hometown, Glen Avon, California, while I was away at BYU my freshman year. I asked her if she knew the Terrill family. She said she did. In fact, she had been one of the missionaries who was instrumental in Brother Terrill's conversion to the Church. I asked her to tell me the story behind his conversion.

She said that the Spirit told her and her companion that brother Terrill knew the gospel was true, but that he just needed to be asked to be baptized. They listened and courageously followed the still, small voice, which told them to challenge him to be baptized. They set a date, told him the font would be full of warm water, and that the Elders would be there, dressed in white, ready to baptize him.

My neighbor then told me of an experience she had with the power of darkness a few days before the baptism. She and her companion were awakened by a spirit of darkness which appeared at the foot of their bed. This spirit-being complained that they were intruding on his area, and told them to stay out! She phoned the zone leaders to come and pronounce a blessing over their proselyting area and to cast out the evil spirit. The priesthood power brought about the desired result in protecting them and their work: Brother Terrill arrived at his baptism, as they had hoped he would.

As I listened to JoAnn's story, I suddenly recognized that all the ugly thoughts I had been experiencing had come from the same kind of evil influence which had manifested itself to the sister missionaries—an influence which was now trying to intrude on *my* area. I realized then that I needed a priesthood blessing to rid me of the evil thoughts which were intruding on my mind and trying to influence me. It took two blessings over the next three months to work through this trial.

I learned from my own experience of the destructive power which the Evil One can exert in our lives by whispering in our ears messages of hate, fear, anger, or any kind of evil influence. In 2 Nephi 28:20–22, Nephi describes Satan's method of influencing the thoughts of men: "He whispereth in their ears, until he grasps them with his awful chains, from whence there is no deliverance."

Elder Joseph Fielding Smith taught, "In his effort to entice, Satan has great power. We should always be on guard to resist Satan's advances. He has power to place thoughts in our minds and to whisper to us unspoken impressions to entice us to satisfy our appetites or desires and in various other ways he plays upon our weaknesses and desires." (*Answers to Gospel Questions*, comp. Joseph Fielding Smith, Jr., Vol. 3, p. 81.)

It is important to note that Satan's power is not unrestrained. Joseph Smith taught that Satan has no more power over us than what we give him. According to the law of moral agency, neither the Holy Ghost nor the Evil One has power to control a person against his will.

Chapter Four

FAITH MAKES POSSIBLE THE MIRACLE OF PERSONAL REVELATION: LEARNING TO LISTEN TO THE SPIRIT

YOU DID NOT COME TO EARTH JUST TO RECEIVE YOUR BODY. YOU came to learn how to solve problems by praying for light and knowledge and by receiving your own personal revelation through the Holy Ghost. Thus, by that means of enlightenment, you awaken to the laws of faith, the laws by which all things are possible and which operate this universe.

Alma 3:26 tells us that "They might reap their rewards according to their works, whether they were good or whether they were bad, to reap eternal happiness or eternal misery, according to the spirit which they listed to obey, whether it be a good spirit or a bad one."

How to Recognize Revelation

There are many voices calling to us in this life and many of the voices are within our own minds. It has been said life's hardest battles are fought within the chambers of the mind. These mental battles do occur—the wrestling within of good versus bad, of inspiration versus "sinspiration." A spirit may indeed speak to a mortal, though it is perceived as a thought or an impression in the mind and is usually heard in the person's own tone of voice. That person may then exercise his moral agency as to what he will do with that thought, whether he will accept or reject it, act on it or not.

Your Two-station Receiving Set

Human beings use electrical energy to transmit messages through telephone, radio, and television. But spirit beings have a better system to communicate with us. They send messages to us through our thoughts; thus, we could say that our brains are spiritual receiving sets for spiritual communication. However, as I have mentioned, there is more than one station which you can listen to. There are two radio-like stations which can speak into your mind: the Lord's station and Satan's station. You can receive thoughts or impressions into your mind from each station. You can receive promptings from God, or you can attune yourself to the negative whisperings of Satan.

How Does the Lord Speak to Us?

The Lord has often made reference to "the voice of my Spirit" (see D&C 97:1), through which he gives personal revelation. This form of communication in the mind and the heart is often referred to as the "still, small voice." Elijah referred to it in 1 Kings 19:13 and Nephi spoke of it in 1 Nephi 17:45. Helaman 5:30 refers to this still, small voice, as does D&C 85:6. In a 1989 October conference address, Elder Boyd K. Packer explained that:

> The Holy Ghost communicates with the spirit through the mind more than through the physical senses. This guidance comes as thoughts and as feelings, through impressions and promptings. It is not always easy to describe inspiration. The scriptures teach us that we may "feel" the words of spiritual communication more than hear them and that we see with spiritual rather than with mortal eyes. The patterns of revelation are not dramatic. The voice of inspiration is a still voice, a small voice.

Elder S. Dilworth Young offers a simple explanation of how this communication takes place. "Then, as needed, according to his wisdom, his word will come into my mind through my thoughts, accompanied by a feeling . . . of peace, a further witness that what one heard is right."

Shortly after his martyrdom, in a spiritual visit to Brigham Young, Joseph Smith commented on the importance of paying heed to the still, small voice and directed Brigham to tell the people to be careful not to turn from the direction of the Spirit.

How Does the Spirit Speak to You?

In order to heed the voice of the Spirit, you must understand how to recognize it and to learn how to be attuned to receiving it. There are a number of ways in which the Spirit can speak to your mind and heart. It is very possible that you may have repeatedly experienced the whisperings of the Spirit and not even been aware that you did (as did the Lamanites spoken of in 3 Nephi 9:20).

An article titled "Have I Received an Answer from the Spirit?" suggests a number of ways in which you may have been prompted by the Spirit. Each of these ways is discussed below.

1. The Spirit speaks peace to the mind.
2. The Spirit causes our bosoms to burn.
3. The Spirit speaks in our minds and in our hearts.
4. The Spirit comes as a voice in the mind.
5. The Spirit leads.
6. The Spirit occupies our minds and presses upon our feelings.
7. The Spirit constrains.

(*Ensign*, April 1989, pp. 21–25.)

1. The Spirit Speaks Peace to the Mind

D&C 6:23 tells how Oliver Cowdery was seeking for a witness from the Lord during the time of the translation of the Book of Mormon. The Lord says: "Did I not speak peace to your mind concerning the matter? What greater witness can you have than from God?"

Feelings such as calmness, peace, and tranquility are, perhaps, the most common manifestations of the Spirit.

The Lord Answered Us—He Will Answer You

The year 1978 was an especially difficult one for my family and me. My husband was diagnosed as having cancer and was given a 60 percent chance to live, and I was frightened. Hans had undergone his first exploratory surgery and was scheduled to go in for his second operation. We were all fasting and praying. I called family members in Canada, Utah, Colorado, and Virginia to fast and pray with us. We also had asked our bishop, Dick Skousen, and our elders quorum president, Jim Jamieson, to administer to Hans. Jim was to be the mouthpiece.

Soon, the first beautiful miracle occurred. My husband was told in the blessing that he would be made well and whole. As I sat listening, the marvelous confirmation of the Spirit came over me—the tingling and burning sensation which D&C 9:8 explains. It enveloped my whole being and I *knew* that everything would be all right. I knew that he would be healed and made whole.

However, troubles still continued to plague us. The hot water heater broke and the roof started to leak. The garbage disposal went out and then the sewer line collapsed! Since our income was used up by the regular necessities of life and by the medical bills we had to pay, this was a very stressful situation.

I felt the heavy burden of depression upon me every moment. The trials seemed more than I could bear. I retired to my prayer room (it was no longer just the bedroom.) I had poured out my heart to the Lord and asked for the trials to stop, yet they continued. I had asked for the wrong thing. So I said, "Wilt thou please take from me the deep burden I feel? Wilt thou take the weight from my tired shoulders, the stress and the tears that have flowed too easily?" That desire was granted and in an instant all depression and sorrow were taken from me and I finally knew peace.

I know God lives and answers prayers. I know how the people in Mosiah 24:10-17 must have felt. Their trials did not cease either, yet they carried their burdens and did not feel them. The Lord told them, "And I will also ease the burdens which are put upon your shoulders, that even you cannot feel them upon your backs, even while you are in bondage; and this will I do that ye may stand as witnesses for me hereafter, and that ye may know of a surety that I, the Lord God, do visit my people in their afflictions." (Mosiah 24:14.)

2. The Spirit Causes Your Bosom (or Inner Soul) to Burn

Perhaps you have experienced a tingling or warm feeling during an inspirational sacrament meeting or when you felt inspired to get up and bear your testimony. This is spoken of in D&C 9:8: "And if it is right I will cause that your bosom shall burn within you; therefore, you shall feel that it is right."

When I offered a salesman named Gary a copy of the Book of Mormon using Elder Hartman Rector Jr.'s idea of asking people, "Do you like to read?" the Spirit confirmed the rightness of this member-missionary effort. I told the salesman how the record gives an account of the visit of Jesus Christ to the Americas, and asked if he would like to read about it if I sent him a copy? He said "yes" and wrote down his name and address on a card for me. When the missionaries delivered the book they presented the salesman with the card he had filled out. He was willing to listen to them. His wife, Janine, was equally interested. Gary and Janine Meaner were baptized on 3 June 1989. We were invited to witness the baptism. Gary was baptized first and ordained a priest so he could baptize his wife. As Janine was being baptized, I felt the burning within and the sweet, tingling presence of the Spirit sweep over my body again—another testimony of the reality of the Spirit and how it works with us.

3. The Spirit Speaks in Your Mind and in Your Heart

When the Holy Ghost speaks, your mind may be struck with insight and clarity and you may have a sudden understanding of the meaning of a passage of scripture or doctrine. This understanding may also come simply as a feeling which says "Yes, that makes sense," or "Now I understand what that means." Another way this understanding may come is in the form of specific instructions.

After my husband's third operation (this time for gall-stones), once more I felt I could not take any more; and again I sent a call for help to the Lord. I felt my reserves had run dry, that I had no more to give. I felt an urgent need to get away with my sweetheart for a while, away from the constant pressure of the children's needs and demands. As I sat on the couch one day, thinking, I allowed my own real needs and desires to flow forth, even though I was sure there was no earthly way for them to be realized. "We need to get away," I said to myself. I don't know whether I spoke it silently or out loud. But I do know I heard a voice spoken in reply. It said, "Yes, you need to get away." I knew I was alone, yet I heard a voice speak to me in my mind.

What a welcome change—someone was agreeing with me! I thought, I don't know who you are, but let's keep talking.

It spoke again: "You need to get away to a cabin."

A cabin? I thought, we can't afford to rent a cabin.

"Just tell someone," the voice responded, "and it will be so."

Less than half an hour later, a friend called to see how I was. We talked for awhile, then she asked me if I needed anything. I remembered that the voice said to share what I had been told, so I did. I replied, "We need to get away to a cabin." My friend replied that she had a friend who had a cabin to rent and perhaps she had an opening. Mentally, I said, "Spirit, I thought this was going to be free!" (We had no money after paying our share of the doctor bills.) I thanked her for her thoughtfulness, and we chatted some more.

Not long after that, Carole Augustine, my visiting teacher stopped by to drop off a much needed item she had picked up for me. As we chatted, she too asked me if there was anything we needed. I thought, "I am not going to use the word cabin again, but I will say something." "We need to get way." Carole's eyes sparkled, "We have a cabin up on Mt. Graham," she said. "You can leave tomorrow and stay as long as you would like." Wonderful, but what about the kids? I thought. As though she had read my mind, she added, "And I'll take care of your children!" What joy and gratitude I felt. I could hardly believe what I had just heard. The Lord, recognizing my desire, had spoken into my mind; this time, he quickly granted my desire. I began to truly understand that the Lord knows our very thoughts and can talk to us through them when we turn to him for help. He speaks to our spirits. Joseph Smith wrote about this:

> All things whatsoever God in his infinite wisdom has seen fit and proper to reveal to us, while we are dwelling in mortality, in regard to our mortal bodies, are revealed to us in the abstract, and independent of affinity of this mortal tabernacle, but are revealed to our spirits precisely as though we had no bodies at all. (*Teachings of The Prophet Joseph Smith*, p.355.)

About this time, I began to understand more of the meaning of the scriptures. I began to see things in the scriptures which I had hardly noticed or understood before. As I studied, certain passages seemed to jump off the page as their meaning became clear to me. They may have been written hundreds or even thousands of years ago, but they were also written for me today. Through the Holy Ghost I was beginning to understand their meaning for me.

In order to fully understand the ways the Spirit speaks to you, you need to understand the way the words "mind" and "heart" are used in the scriptures. The words "heart," "mind," and "thoughts" are used interchangeably in the scriptures, just as they are sometimes used in common speech. This can cause confusion as we read the scriptures. What does the Lord mean when he speaks of the heart and mind? You can begin to understand the connection between mind and heart (your thoughts and your feelings) when you understand that thoughts trigger emotions in your body. When you feel emotion, how do you describe where you feel it? You say you feel it in your heart.

The word "heart" describes the entire experience, which involves thoughts and emotions. The words "thought" and "mind" usually denote only the thinking part of an experience. When you receive positive or enlightening thoughts from the Lord in your mind, you start to feel his influence and you say you feel it in your heart. The thought comes into your mind. Then the thymus, an endocrine gland located under the sternum, registers and stores the emotion caused by thoughts. Dr. John Diamond, an M.D. and a psychiatrist, explains that "the thymus is the first organ of the body to be affected by stress. It is also the first organ to be affected at an energy level by an emotional state. The thymus gland may thus be thought of as the link between mind and body." (*Your Body Doesn't Lie*, p. 62.) According to Karen Bulloch, who directs the neuroimmune program at the University of San Diego, there is evidence that "the brain and the immune system communicate with each other. . . . Nerve fibers [were found] in the thymus gland, an organ underneath the breastbone that produces immune blood cells, or T-cells." (*Reader's Digest*, Sept. 1989.) Further,

> David Felten at the University of Rochester School of Medicine also traced nerve fibers to the thymus, spleen, lymph nodes and bone marrow—all parts of the immune system. Since all nerves are ultimately linked to the brain, the work by these scientists documents a clear connection. (*Reader's Digest*, Sept. 1989.)

I believe that the function of the thymus gives us a physical explanation for emotion (caused by thought) being felt as a burning in the bosom. Apparently, the thymus registers the emotion and then stores it in the tissues of the body. We say that this phenomenon occurs in the heart.

Substituting the words "heart" or "mind" with the words "thoughts" or "emotions" can give us a greater understanding of what we are reading. Let us use the following scriptures as examples:

> And there was no inequality among them; the Lord did pour out his Spirit on all the face of the land to prepare the minds of the children of men, or to prepare their hearts to receive the word which should be taught among them at the time of his coming. (Alma 16:16.)

Notice how Alma uses the words "mind" and "heart" interchangeably. Sometimes these words may be symbolic. In order to understand, you need to pray to know the Lord's meaning so you can comprehend the symbolism. In this case, the word "heart" probably refers to more than the thoughts. The word "heart" is used to show that the Lord intends to prepare them emotionally as well as mentally.

In the following scriptures, the word "heart" most likely means "mind."

> Therefore, verily I say unto you, lift up your voices unto this people; speak the thoughts that I shall put into your *hearts*, and you shall not be confounded before men. (D&C 100:5; italics added.)

> And it came to pass that he commanded the multitude that they should cease to pray, and also his disciples. And he commanded them that they should not cease to pray in their *hearts*. (3 Nephi 20:1; italics added.)

4. The Spirit Comes as a Voice in the Mind

The experience of hearing a voice instructing me that if I would tell someone we needed to get away to a cabin, that it would be so, was a particularly memorable example of how the Spirit speaks as a voice in the mind. The following experience also illustrates this point.

Some time after the cabin experience, my husband was scheduled to have radiation treatments. We knew taking care of him and all of the children at the same time would be too difficult for me to do alone. The instruction was placed in my mind to talk to fellow members of my Relief Society stake board. I did as I was instructed and within twenty-four hours, two rides became available to us—kind friends who offered to take our four oldest children to Utah to their grandparents' house for four weeks. This meant many hours of travel for these people, but our need was great, and through kind, loving people who responded to our need, the Lord provided a way to free us from the stress we were feeling.

5. The Spirit Leads

At no time will Satan lead someone to do good, so you can be certain of the source of promptings to do good. This is expressed in Moroni 7:17: "He persuadeth no man to do good, no, not one." As recorded in D&C 11:12, Hyrum Smith was told to "put your trust in that Spirit which leadeth to do good—yea, to do justly, to walk humbly, to judge righteously; and this is my Spirit." Pure impressions stay positive, pure, and enlightening. They stay in line with the true patterns which our leaders have taught us.

6. The Spirit Occupies Your Mind and Presses upon Your Feelings

A vivid illustration of this is recorded in D&C 128:1. In an epistle to the Church, Joseph Smith expresses his concerns about the baptism for the dead. He said, "I now resume the subject of baptism for the dead, as that subject seems to occupy my mind, and press itself upon my feelings the strongest."

7. The Spirit Constrains

Constrain means to warn against or restrain. Many instances are recorded about people feeling an inner warning to discontinue a certain course. When they heeded this feeling or voice, they either avoided some disaster or were told that they were blessed for obeying the Spirit. One well-known story is of Wilford Woodruff who had scheduled passage on a boat along with some Saints he was bringing from New England and Canada to the West. The Spirit spoke to Elder Woodruff and told him that neither he nor his company should go aboard the boat. He obeyed and told the Saints they should wait for the next boat. The boat left. Some fifty yards downstream, it caught fire and sank.

Alma 14:11 gives an illustration of an instance when someone was blessed for obeying the Spirit. Alma tells Amulek, who wanted Alma to exercise the power of God to save the people from the flames, that "The spirit constraineth me that I must not stretch forth mine hand; for behold the Lord receiveth them up unto himself, in glory; and he doth suffer that they may do this thing . . . that the judgments which he shall exercise upon them in his wrath may be just."

8. The Spirit Often Brings You to Tears

Brigham Young said that when the Spirit is felt, you cannot withhold the tears. I believe this is the reason we are often unable to hold back the tears when we are bearing our testimonies. Tears that accompany positive peaceful feelings are often another manifestation of the truth or righteousness of some idea or desire.

9. The Spirit Can Save Your Life If It Is the Will of the Lord

When Brigham Smoot left for his mission to Samoa, he promised his mother that he would not go swimming because he did not know how to swim. However, since this was the only method of bathing that was in general use in Samoa, his companion soon persuaded him to bathe in the sea with all the other elders. As the new elder was wading out, he fell into a deep hole in the reef.

Elder Wood had promised to be responsible for the new elder's safety and, noticing his absence, he began a frantic search. Brigham was soon found in the attitude of prayer at the bottom of the hole. His limp body was dragged from the hole and carried to the beach. Elder Wood said of his companion, "He was perfectly lifeless and dead." In vain, the elders used all normal restorative measures.

By this time, a large crowd of inquisitive natives had gathered around. Their story of a native boy who had previously drowned in the same hole brought no comfort to the worried missionaries.

At this time, Elder Wood said he felt inspired by the Spirit that the only way to restore his companion's life was to administer to him. The superstitious natives warned against such treatment of the body and thought it sacrilegious to tamper with life and death.

They were obedient to the inspiration, however, and they anointed Elder Smoot's head with oil. While Elder

Wood was sealing the anointing he felt life come back into Elder Smoot's body. Shortly after the administration, Elder Smoot talked with the missionaries and bore solemn testimony to them of how in the spirit, he watched them recover his body from the hole, take it to the beach, and try to restore it to life. He told of touching Elder Wood on the shoulder and telling him that the only way to bring life back to his body was to use the priesthood which he bore. (*Samoan Mission Journal*, 18 June 1889.)

You Are a Spiritual Receiving Set

You are literally a spiritual receiving set; you are able to hear and respond to spiritual communications from beings you cannot see. You receive spiritual information in the form of thoughts and ideas (most of the time in your own tone of voice). The mind becomes an instrument of the spirit. Difficulty arises because Satan can also put thoughts into your mind. Elder Boyd K. Packer had this to say about "negative inspiration" or "sinspiration":

All inspiration does not come from God. The evil one has power to tap into those channels of revelation and send conflicting signals which can mislead and confuse us. There are promptings from evil sources which are so carefully counterfeited as to deceive even the very elect. Nevertheless, we can learn to discern these spirits. (*Ensign*, Nov. 1989, p. 14.)

Chapter Five

APPLYING THE PRINCIPLES

IN ETHER 3:2 WE READ, "NEVERTHELESS, O LORD, THOU HAS GIVEN us a commandment that we must call upon thee, that from thee we may receive according to our desires." This alone should awaken a desire in you to learn the laws of faith. Where do you begin to use them in the right ways?

The process seems to be as follows: first you program your mind with positive thoughts and ideas about Christ by study and prayer until you no longer doubt that Christ lives. Then your righteous desires, confirmed by the Spirit, point the way to the miracles which will eventually come to pass due to your single-minded prayers of faith to the Lord. There seem to be ten steps that work best for me as I attempt to actively apply the principles of faith:

The Ten Steps of Faith

1. Recognize a desire or a challenge.

2. Think and ponder about how you desire to solve the challenge. Pray for light and knowledge in regard to its accomplishment. Now ideas can come from the Spirit into your mind. Listen and immediately do whatever the Spirit directs you to do.

3. Choose a desire and then ask: "Is this desire for my good?" You may feel a positive emotional impression, a feeling of "yes" within you, or even better, the burning or tingling of the Spirit. You may feel a

negative impression or a stupor of thought which indicates a "no." Correct the request until you receive a "yes" confirmation. (See D&C 46:7-9, 23, 30.)

4. Wait for the answer. Answers come in many ways:

—A burning in the soul. (D&C 9:8.)

—Instructions received as thoughts in the mind. (D&C 8:2–4; Enos 1:10.)

—Feelings of peace. (D&C 6:22–23.)

—Instructions in dreams.

—Positive ideas which stay in the mind. (D&C 128:1.)

5. If the Spirit confirms your desire, it becomes God's will for you, "wherefore it is done even as he asketh." (D&C 46:30.) Now, write it down.

6. Use the following procedure to spiritually release the confirmed desire into the Lord's hands. Ask:

—"Would I release this confirmed desire to the Lord?" (Answer "yes.").

—"Could I release it by my faith in Jesus Christ to help me? (Answer "yes.")

—"When will I let it go into the Lord's hands and release it to be fulfilled in the Lord's own time for me?" (Answer "now.")

Now do the following:

—In your prayers say, "I thank thee for the (name what you are asking for) which is coming. (In this statement, you are saying that you are hoping for something you do not see which the Spirit has confirmed.)

—Doubt not in your heart or thoughts.

—Be aware that your faith will be tried at this time through negative thoughts or situations.

—Say, "I choose to release these negative thoughts," or use the "Would I?" "Could I?" "When?" procedure.

—Now, listen to the positive ideas or impressions from the Spirit as it guides you and do what it confirms.

7. Persist in prayer and follow the impressions of the Spirit until you receive your confirmed desire.

8. According to the Lord's timetable, you shall receive your desire through your faith in Jesus Christ.

9. Feel the joy of having your righteous desires come to pass or reflect on what you can learn when they do not come to pass.

10. Give thanks in all things and start again.

By this procedure, I do not mean to imply that you should submit your order to the Lord, and then put your life on hold, focusing all your energy into the request until he delivers it. Instead, determine a righteous desire, then persist peacefully in faith and prayer as you continue with your life. It is also a misunderstanding to assume that you choose one desire and avoid approaching the Lord with any other until that one is fulfilled. It may be that the goal or righteous desire you have chosen to focus on will not be fulfilled until the Millennium! The idea is to consistently determine many righteous desires to present to the Lord in faith, and then to trust in the Lord's timetable for their fulfillment.

This is only one clear pattern through which the Lord can work with you. You may follow the example of others who have used these and many other laws of faith and were blessed with joy for doing so.

Missionaries in North Germany Ask, Seek, and Knock

Sisters Carrie Roquemore of Brighton, Colorado, and Kimberly Batchelor of Mesa, Arizona served together for a number of months. Both were eager to learn, grow, and build their understanding of the gospel so that they might have a rich and rewarding mission. They decided they could best do so by concentrating on faith, the first principle of the gospel. I quote from their letter to me:

As Sister Batchelor and I began our intense study of faith, we began to listen to your tape, "Faith Unpuzzled," every day. We also began to find a lot of information in the scriptures and in other books. Whenever we'd find something of interest or significance during our personal study, we'd share it and discuss it. As our understanding deepened, we noticed something happening to us. Faith was no longer something mysterious that just happened. We were beginning to see that the level of our faith was directly dependent on our understanding of the workings of faith and what we did with that understanding. We were in control! What a heady sensation that was! We could do something about it!

As we applied the simple steps and exercises we learned from our study, and as we took upon ourselves direct responsibility for our thoughts, and consequently our actions, the miracles started occurring. The principles we followed were:

1. Watch over your thoughts and practice mentally erasing all negative thoughts and replacing them with positive thoughts.
2. Write out your desires and ask if they are the Lord's will.
3. When the Spirit reveals that they are for your good, persist in prayer until you receive them.
4. Mentally cast out all doubting thoughts in order to focus on your most persistent thought. As you do this, you are doing your part; the Lord can now do his part, for you are being single-minded!

Some people say the North Germans are a cold people. I can understand why there is this misconception. When we did street contacting, most often the people would simply walk by without acknowledging our existence. Many times they were rude and brusque. But as we began applying ourselves to the task of controlling our thoughts, keeping them positive, seeing only the good, and pushing away and eventually clearing the negative influences, a wonderful thing happened. Not only did our love for these people grow deeper and purer, that same love entered our companionship. We made our own discovery, that this positive mind-set leads to a well of pure Christlike love. And, of course, everyone around us could feel it, too.

As we applied our positive faith to our proselyting skills, the people responded beautifully. Before we knew it, we had over thirty new people in our teaching pool simply because of our increased faith and knowledge that this was the Lord's work and that he would bless us with success.

One day, during an incredible cold snap, we bundled up to do our regular morning street contacting followed by tracting in apartment buildings. From previous experience, we knew mornings were not a good time to tract, and we were loathe to give up our street contacting. Even though there was the possibility of frozen limbs, we decided to talk to just a few more people.

The Lord blessed us because of our determination. The next person we talked to was a mother with two children in tow. She stopped readily and immediately invited us over to talk to her and her husband the next Saturday. She was a beautiful woman who had been looking into every religion searching for the truth. She suffered several traumatic blows in her personal life not long after hearing our message and could have become disillusioned or disheartened, but she kept the faith and accepted the baptismal challenge.

As we became more confident in our understanding of faith and our ability to call upon it, we decided to take up a challenge by President Taylor. He told us we should not only pray to be led to those chosen and ready brothers and sisters, but that we should pray to have them led to us! When I first heard that statement, I remember thinking, "yeah, right!" But now it didn't seem at all unrealistic. We took Elder Taylor's challenge to heart and within the first few days two young women came up to us and asked us if we could come and tell them more about the Church. The principle of faith at work is really powerful!

Sincerely,
Sister Roquemore
Sister Batchelor

How Can I Lay Hold on Every Good Thing?

And now, my brethren, how is it possible that ye can lay hold on every good thing?

And now I come to that faith, of which I said I would speak; and I will tell you the way whereby ye may lay hold on every good thing.

Wherefore, by the ministering of angels, and by every word that proceeded forth out of the mouth of God, men began to exercise faith in Christ; and thus by faith, they did lay hold upon every good thing; and thus it was until the coming of Christ.

And after that he came men also were saved by faith in his name; and by faith, they become the sons of God. And as sure as Christ liveth he spake these words unto our fathers, saying: Whatsoever thing ye shall ask the Father in my name, which is good, in faith believing that ye shall receive, behold, it shall be done unto you. (Moroni 7:20, 21, 25, 26.)

Having faith in Christ is the first step for you to "lay hold on every good thing." What else must you do to discover your righteous desires? The above scripture gives us the steps. First, you must ask! How must you ask? You must ask in the name of Christ.

These three words are the key to the next step: "which is good." How do you know what is good? This step involves gaining a confirmation from the Spirit that your desire is good, meaning good for you—only the Lord knows for sure what is good for you because he has the eternal perspective.

Then too, we must look at the reality that a righteous desire that might appear to be nothing *but* good for you, may not be possible in the present because of the choices of others. One woman learned this principle through many years of wrong application. She fasted and prayed and exerted all her faith to the goal of having her husband change. She *knew* it would be good for her if he would put more priority on the family and be more loving. She could not imagine that it could be anything other than the Lord's will. Yet her husband did not change—in fact, he became a more and more negative influence in their home. At her wits end, she tearfully pleaded with the Lord for understanding. "Why ? Why? Why?" she asked. The Lord gave her the answer in her mind: "Free agency."

Suddenly she realized that she had been giving the Lord an unrighteous request. He has promised to honor our free agency at all costs, yet she wanted the Lord to change her husband against his will. She realized she should have been focusing her faith and energies on how *she* could change and overcome her own weaknesses.

It is righteous to pray for increased spiritual influence of a loved one, and to ask for other people to be placed in his path—people who might touch that person's heart. It is also good to ask the Lord to put positive spiritual messages into that person's mind. Yet we must honor people's right to decide what they will do with those messages. As we persist in these things and follow the Spirit, we can be at peace, knowing the Lord is in charge and that we have done our best in the situation.

Let us examine in more detail the steps we must take to discover our righteous desires.

The Lord's Most Frequent Instruction

The Lord tells us that we are to pray. In D&C 29:6 he says, "And, as it is written—Whatsoever ye shall ask in faith, being united in prayer according to my command, ye shall receive." We are to pray for that which we desire and which we feel is needful for our well-being. It need not even be a spoken hope or desire; it can be one which is mentally sent out in our thoughts. The Lord can hear it even if it is a prayer spoken only in our minds, offered to him when we cannot speak aloud. In Mosiah 24:12, we read of Alma and his people who were being persecuted by the wicked priest, Amulon, and who were not even allowed to pray vocally. Yet they continued to pray unto God in their hearts, "and he did know the thoughts of their hearts."

On every occasion when the Prophet Joseph Smith received revelation, he first had to ask because of his desire to know. You also have to ask first to receive. The Lord can only work through your prayers of faith. He must wait for you to awaken to his power before he links your prayers of faith to his power.

Matthew 7:7-11 is one of many scriptures which tell us what we must do to receive help from the Lord.

Ask [for light and knowledge], and it shall be given you; seek, and ye shall find; knock, and it shall be opened unto you:

For every one that asketh receiveth; and he that seeketh findeth; and to him that knocketh it shall be opened.

Or what man is there of you, whom if his son ask bread, will he give him a stone?

Or if he ask a fish, will he give him a serpent?

If ye then, being evil, know how to give good gifts unto your children, how much more shall your Father which is in heaven give good things to them that ask him?

The most frequent instruction the Lord has given us is that we should ask, seek, and knock. This means that he cannot bless us unless we ask.

A Miracle in Douglas, Arizona

Ann Harvey shares this experience:

In August of 1989, I began to feel inspired that we should move from Douglas to Mesa. We had been trying to sell our home in Douglas for over a year with no success. I came across some information written by Carolyn Ringger on how to use faith. As I read, I felt sure that this was the way for us to go. As a family, we discussed the principle of "asking in faith" and began to pray together and individually for the "righteous desire" to sell our home and move to Mesa. This was confirmed as the will of the Lord for us.

In December, we sold our house! In January, we moved to Mesa. Our miracle had come to pass by our faith in Jesus Christ! But the challenges of earth life continued when, in April, our ten-year-old daughter was diagnosed as having cancer. She had shown symptoms of anemia for a year, but the doctor in Sierra Vista had not been able to find the cause of her problem.

She has since recovered from surgery and has shown no signs of any recurrence of the cancer. My husband is convinced that if we had not been able to get to the doctors in the children's hospital in Phoenix (which we couldn't do when we lived in Douglas), our daughter would not be alive today. Our miracle move to Mesa opened the doors for other miracles.

This was just the beginning of the miracles that have unfolded in my life in the past two years because I have applied the laws of faith.

Counsel with the Lord

In Alma 37:37, the Lord tells us to "Counsel with the Lord in all thy doings, and he will direct thee for good; yea, when thou liest down at night lie down unto the Lord, that he may watch over you in your sleep; and when thou risest in the morning let thy heart be full of thanks unto God."

Does that mean we should ask him even about our small material affairs such as that mundane daily problem, that needed piece of furniture, that job, or that snarl in our household affairs? The Lord says that it is.

Even Plants Matter to the Lord If They Matter to Me

Even little things matter! I desired some green plants to beautify our home. I realized I now had the courage to ask for something that unimportant. I prayed, "Father, may I ask for some plants for our home? There is no money in the budget for them. But may I ask for them and ask for thy help to receive them?" The Spirit impressed within me, "Yes, you may ask for them; they are for your good."

I wrote "I thank thee for our green plants" on my desire list. I presented the confirmed desire to the Lord in my prayers and doubted not that it would soon be given to me because the Spirit had spoken.

One day the instruction came to my mind: "Go to Frys' Grocery Store." My first thought was, "I don't want to go to Frys'." The inner instruction came again. Finally, I discerned that the thought impressions were from the Spirit. So, I went to Frys', curious to know why I had been sent there. There I saw a number of philodendron plants on the floor which looked rather yellow. I knew water would revive them. My next impression was that they were going to be marked down. "Go talk to the manager" the inner voice impression said, so I followed the instructions. I asked him if the plants were going to be marked down. "Yes," he said. "How much would you like to pay for them?" I bought twenty plants for a dollar each using baby-sitting money I had just received. We still have eleven of the plants today, my constant reminder that the Lord loves me and that my small desires *do* matter to him.

This was a marvelous revelation to me. Even plants matter to the Lord if they matter to me. So I started writing down what we needed. I would then present a need to the Lord and ask if it was for our good. The Spirit would confirm, and time after time our needs were fulfilled at a price we could afford to pay. (I want to make it clear that this did not always happen instantaneously. For example, it took nine months of persistent prayer and exercise of our faith before a way was open for me to get the computer I needed. Other things that I have been praying about for years have not occurred. But I have learned to trust in the Lord's timetable and to not demand that he accept mine.) Each day I would ask only for those items that the Spirit had confirmed. Then I would thank the Lord throughout the day that this blessing would be coming to pass. If doubting thoughts came, I would talk back to them. I would say, "I choose to clear these thoughts. I have my own agency," and they would leave my mind. Now I easily remove all negative thought by using the "Would I? Could I? When?" procedure discussed previously. I also release the confirmed desires into the Lord's hands as is described in step six of the "Ten Steps of Faith."

It is wise to use the moments of the day when you are not required to deal with other things to mentally focus on the laws of faith. Ponder them. Study them out in your mind. And keep a prayer in your heart all day. Think about your hopes and desires and focus on the things you are praying for. This will help your faith to become spontaneous and natural.

Study It Out in Your Mind

When you pray to ask for a blessing, and you follow the steps we have just mentioned, is that all that is required, or is there something more? This has been a question which has concerned the people of God since the time of

Adam. It was one of the requests made of Christ by his Apostles shortly before his death: "Lord, teach us to pray." (Luke 11:1.)

An excellent answer to this question was given to us in modern revelation. Oliver Cowdery had been helping the Prophet Joseph Smith with the translation of the Book of Mormon. Oliver desired to do some translation so he asked the prophet. The prophet inquired of the Lord whether to allow him to do so. Oliver was granted this privilege. However, he did not understand what was required in order to exercise this gift, and it was taken away from him. In Section 9:7-9 of the Doctrine and Covenants, the Lord explains to him why his righteous desires were not fulfilled:

> Behold you have not understood; you have supposed that I would give it unto you, when you took no thought save it was to ask me.
>
> But, behold, I say unto you, that you must study it out in your mind; then you must ask me if it be right, and if it is right I will cause that your bosom shall burn within you; therefore, you shall feel that it is right.
>
> But if it be not right you shall have no such feelings, but you shall have a stupor of thought.

This very important step of prayer is sometimes misunderstood, yet you cannot expect to receive a blessing from the Lord unless you have studied it out in your mind and know what it is that you want from the Lord.

What Will Ye that I Should Do?

The story of the brother of Jared is a good example of this principle. We learn in Ether 2:23-25 that when the brother of Jared needed light for his boats, he presented the problem to the Lord. The Lord simply said, "What will ye that I should do that ye may have light in your vessels?"

The brother of Jared understood what he must do in order to receive answers from the Lord. He went up into the mountain and no doubt did some studying and pondering. Then, the scriptures tell us, he:

Did molten out of a rock sixteen small stones; and they were white and clear, even as transparent as glass; and he did carry them in his hands upon the top of the mount, and cried again unto the Lord, saying:

O Lord, . . . thou has given us a commandment that we must call upon thee, that from thee we may receive according to our desires.

And I know, O Lord, that thou hast all power, and can do whatsoever thou wilt for the benefit of man; therefore touch these stones, O Lord, with thy finger, and prepare them that they may shine forth in darkness . . . that we may have light while we shall cross the sea. (Ether 3:1-2, 4.)

The Lord honored the brother of Jared's request because he studied the problem out in his mind when he was instructed to do so. Then he went back to the Lord in faith with a specific request. He worked out a plan, took the action required, and acknowledged his need for the Lord's help and his confidence in the Lord's power. The Lord then confirmed his plan and answered his prayer. He offered his prayer in total faith, doubting not that the Lord could do all things. He knew, therefore, that his request could be granted and he was single-minded in his belief—he did not doubt!

How marvelous for us to recognize that, in reality, this scripture is giving us a pattern to follow. The Lord is asking us to think for ourselves what we want him to do for us. Then we are to ask him for that help in single-minded faith.

Answers to Personal Concerns

In 1986, just after our son Eric graduated from high school, we received word that he was to receive the Presidential Scholar Award on the White House lawn, along with selected students from each of the other states. I desired with my whole soul to be able to go see him and be there for such a once-in-a-lifetime experience. As I pondered how my faith could help my desire come to pass, a plan began to shape in my mind. Six months earlier, I had been invited by Bunny Whitney, owner of the This Is The

Place bookstore, to speak in the Washington, D.C. area. But, so far, nothing had worked out.

I went to the Lord in sincere prayer and asked him if it would be for the good of all to ask Bunny to help me go there to speak so that my expenses would be provided. The Spirit confirmed my request. I prayed again and told the Lord specifically what I needed for this miracle to come about: money for a ticket, a place to stay, and transportation while I was there. After I finished praying, I immediately felt impressed to call Bunny and explain my situation to her. She quickly caught the idea and started to explain how she thought it could work. She offered to house me and drive me to the White House each day. An inexpressible joy filled my heart as I saw all my needs fulfilled.

Our many trials really can fine-tune our ability to use our faith. We can hear and follow promptings in normal day-to-day life instead of calling upon the Lord only in crisis situations.

I was able to go see Eric and to experience with him this great event in his life. I saw President Reagan and felt the spirit of our country there on the grounds of the White House with all of its history.

On the second day in Washington, D.C., the parents were free to tour the historic sights of the area. I wanted to go to Mt. Vernon where I could walk the same paths George Washington walked. Another reason I wanted to be at that peaceful place was to pursue the answer to a question that was weighing down my mind.

I crossed the acres of the estate, past the carriage house, the smoke house, and the velvet-green pastures where horses still trotted.

I could feel the Spirit close as I asked, "Lord, am I doing what thou wouldst have me do with my life?" I pondered, listening for the still, small voice of the Spirit to give me an answer as it had done so many times before. I knew I had to continue to ask until I received a definite answer. I continued to walk, pondering deeply. Again and again I asked, "Lord, am I doing what thou wouldst have me do? Am I doing what is thy will?"

As I passed Washington's home to my left, with its acres of green lawns, and walked toward the Potomac, I exerted my faith with all my might. Within my heart I cried again to the Lord, "Father am I doing thy will? I ask thee in the name of thy Son, Jesus Christ."

It was then, after a great deal of mental effort on my part, that I heard the familiar still, small voice again. "Yes, my dear daughter," the impressions came, "you are doing what I would have you do." Then it continued, "Please turn around and look toward the home. Now look at those two towering trees on your left. Those trees were planted 200 years ago by the Washington family. They were just tiny seedlings when they were planted, yet look at the size and strength of them now. You, my dear daughter, are also planting seeds—seeds of knowledge of the laws of faith and how they can work. Just as these huge trees have grown, so shall the seeds of knowledge which you are now planting grow and increase." Tears of joy filled my eyes and rolled down my cheeks.

Too often, we sit around and say, "Thy will be done" because we do not want to make the effort to find an answer ourselves. Life would be much easier if we could just have the Lord tell us what to do. But the Lord requires us to study out the problem and tell him what we need so he can help us.

We have our agency and he cannot take that away from us. He does not force mankind. We must do the choosing. He waits for us. Working problems out for ourselves is a necessary part of this earth experience. If all we had to do was take a problem to the Lord and ask him to solve it for us, we would miss the learning process. Sometimes, we act as if the Lord requires us to hurt, when, in fact, hurt is only an indication that we need to focus our attention on an area of our lives and ask the Lord to help us. When we do this, changing a problem into a miracle is often possible.

Here is an account, given by Brother Theodore M. Burton, of the First Quorum of the Seventy, which explains how he developed a better understanding of how the Lord works with us. This was published in the November 1985 *Ensign*, p. 64.

I was called to be a General Authority twenty-five years ago and had no idea at first what I would be asked to do. I was assigned to hold a stake conference the very next weekend and went for advice to my former stake president, Elder Harold B. Lee, who was then a member of the Council of the Twelve Apostles. I asked him to tell me what to do. His answer both shocked and frightened me. He said, "Theodore, you are a General Authority now. No one tells a General Authority how to act in his special calling. If you have questions, ask the Lord and he will instruct you." I had prayed before, never expecting a direct answer, but now I prayed soberly and with real intent.

The Lord did answer my prayers—not in ways I expected, but by speaking things into my mind. But that only happened after I had studied the problem and prepared myself to receive an answer. I have been startled by some of the things that have come to me. Scriptures I had not understood before suddenly were made meaningful. Answers I had previously passed over in reading the scriptures took on new significance. I have truly learned over these years line upon line and precept upon precept. I have learned to follow living prophets as well as those prophets who have passed on. Of necessity, I have learned to live by faith.

Is This Desire for My Good?

But ye are commanded in all things to ask of God, who giveth liberally; and that which the Spirit testifies unto you even so I would that ye should do in all holiness of heart, walking uprightly before me, considering the end of your salvation, doing all things with prayer and thanksgiving, that ye may not be seduced by evil spirits, or doctrines of devils, or the commandments of men; for some are of men, and others of devils. (D&C 46:7.)

D&C 46:30 is also a marvelous and powerful scripture for us to understand. It teaches that: "He that asketh in the Spirit asketh according to the will of God; wherefore it is done even as he asketh." You can take your righteous desires to the Lord at home (and to the temple, at times) to get a confirmation by the Spirit. You may receive a witness in different ways. At times it may be a burning in the soul or a tingling feeling. Other times a positive impression may confirm your request, or you may hear the inner still, small voice which actually speaks by impressions which turn into thoughts you hear in your own inner tone of voice. The common result is that when the Spirit confirms your request, you will know it is right for you to work toward that request and that it is a righteous goal. We never know whether the request will be granted in just the way we expect. Usually, it is not. Many times a confirmed request turns out totally different than we think we want, yet still is for our best good. When the results of a request are not what we desire, many times the long-range effect will be much greater blessings than we could have ever thought to ask for ourselves. Yet, deprived in the moment of a dream, it is far too easy to feel disillusioned and even angry at the Lord. It is important to remember that he always has something even better in mind. "When the good Lord closes a door, he nearly always opens a window," someone said. That window may give us a view of the most important lessons in our lives.

One young woman became engaged in her senior year of high school. Her fiancé was planning to go on a mission the following year, and she agreed to wait for him. She planned to attend college while he was gone. Every time she prayed about her engagement, she felt great about it. She felt absolutely certain that the Lord approved of their decision and that everything would work out for them. She waited faithfully for the entire two-year period, during which time she was busy and happy. She never doubted for a minute that she would marry "her missionary." Just weeks before his return, he called off the engagement. He never even came to see her when he got home. She agonized over her situation—how could the Lord tell her it was right, then pull it out of her reach? Why had she felt so good about it? A roommate who knew her well suggested a possible answer, "Could the

Lord tell you, 'It will be good for you to believe in this engagement but it won't work out?' It was a good growing experience for you and you learned to see boys as friends, free of the pressure of seeing them as potential dates. So maybe that's the only way you could have had the experiences you needed at this stage of your life." Her explanation made sense, and comforted this young woman's heart. She was later able to see many reasons that the marriage would not have been for her best good, but that the engagement *was* for her best good.

Arlene Bascom, a friend of mine from Orem, Utah, shared the following true-life experience with me.

About ten years ago, my husband was having a difficult time with a supervisor at work. We knew it was important for him to change jobs even though jobs were difficult to find during that period of recession. He finally found a job as personnel manager for a newly formed company—a job that paid a good salary and had wonderful potential. But we were extremely hesitant because of the high incidence of failure among new businesses. Also, accepting the job meant moving from the home we had lived in for twenty years, uprooting our family, and taking them to a new community; this is never easy when you have teenagers.

After much prayer, we decided to accept the job. We then asked the Lord to confirm our decision. After praying and fasting, both of us felt good about accepting the job. We were surprised at what we were about to do because we have never been risk-taking people. However, we could not deny that we had received a confirmation of the decision.

The new job lasted less than three weeks, at which time the company folded because of lack of funds. We asked ourselves over and over why we had felt such peace about our decision to accept the job. Though Gary had to struggle for eleven months to find another job, we never lacked anything we really needed during that time.

Looking back on the experience, we could see that the decision was right for two reasons. First, it was important for Gary to get out of the situation he was in at work, at a time when no other opening was available. Second, during that trying time, we experienced many evidences of the

Savior's love for us. We now know without any doubt that he cares about us and that he will take care of us if we rely on him and ask for his help. We could not have learned this lesson if the job had turned out the way we had hoped it would. This experience also taught us that the confirmation of a desire does not necessarily mean that things will turn out exactly as we expect them to!

Learning to receive confirmations is a constant process that requires us to act in faith over and over. It can be hard to tell the difference between our own desires and the Lord's confirmation. Even when we are certain we have received a confirmation, this never means that all will occur as we want, when we want, exactly as we envision. A confirmation only means that a decision will get us going down the right path.

When Our Faith Is Tried

It is a trial of our faith to have a confirmed request not granted or granted in an entirely different way than we expect, as in the Bascom story.

Our faith is also tried when we think we are asking for righteous desires, and later realize we are asking "amiss." James 4:3 says, "Ye ask, and receive not, because ye ask amiss." Conversely, sometimes we are not asking amiss, but we are asking for blessings to be given according to our timetable instead of the Lord's. It is a trial of our faith when a desire is not fulfilled for years, even decades, after we receive a confirmation from the Lord, though we wanted to believe the Lord's "yes" answer meant "yes—today, or tomorrow, at the latest." Our faith is also tried when we feel we are living all the laws of faith—when we believe with nothing wavering—and yet we are deprived of confirmed desires.

Megan Thompson's story can help us understand situations when something we desperately want seems confirmed, but doesn't happen as we expect. She and her husband, who had only daughters, had yearned to adopt a son because Megan could have no more children. Her story is included below.

One cold January afternoon, I received a phone call that led my husband and I to information about a three-year-old boy who needed a home. We were sent a picture of him, and we both fell in love with this brown-eyed, brown-haired, dimpled boy who looked like a twin of our three-year-old daughter, Alice. I immediately called Ben's social worker to ask if he was still available to be adopted. She said they already had three eligible families to present to the selection council. When I had received similar information about other children I had said good-bye and thought, "Well, not this time around." But instead of feeling I should let it go, I told the social worker, Shawna, that I was looking forward to working with her more. She restated that Ben was "taken," but then paused and said, "A strange thing happened three months ago, however. We had selected three families, but at the last minute, two of the three backed out and we didn't feel right about the third." I hung up the phone and looked at the picture of Benjamin on the bulletin board and experienced a feeling of hope.

That night in family prayer, we made our first request of many for Ben to come to our home if it was the Lord's will. The next morning I prayed again for Ben in my personal prayer. I felt deeply impressed that I should ask if this request was right. I was reminded of D&C 9:8, which says, "Then you must ask me if it be right," yet I was hesitant to do so. Up to this point, I had not needed to really exercise my faith. If I could simply say, "Thy will be done," nothing was required of me. When I tried to continue my prayer, the impression returned and finally I prayed, "Is it right for Ben to be a part of our family?" I tried to totally clear my mind and wait for an answer. Then I clearly saw Ben's face in my mind and I felt a surging, joyous hope; I felt the answer was a resounding "Yes!" At that moment, I became fully committed to exerting all my faith, doubting not. I also felt motivated to invite others to add their faith and prayers to ours. I posted pictures of Ben throughout the house and gave some to friends and relatives. I asked them to pray that Ben would be allowed to come to our home because I felt I had received a confirmation that he should be part of our family. Although my husband was doubtful, my desire to have Ben live with us and be little Alice's twin grew and grew.

Every day we prayed to know what we could do to bring about the miracle and every day we were led to do something more. My husband, Tom, was concerned because the free agency of many other people had a bearing on the realization of this miracle; but I assured him that the Lord had given me the confirmation that it was right. The more I looked at the picture, the more my love for Ben grew. The look in his eyes and his bright countenance assured me that he was one of God's elect and that he would respond when we taught him the gospel. (I had reason to believe that none of the other three families would give him that opportunity.)

I had a wonderful experience at the temple the day the council was held. Because of the deep peace I felt while I was there, I felt assured that the windows of heaven had opened and that because of our faith, Ben would be assigned to our family.

The next day I waited for the joyous news. It didn't come. At 4:00 P.M. I called Shawna. She replied, "It's over. One of the other three families I presented to the council yesterday was chosen. Ben will soon be placed with his new family." I managed to say good-bye. For a moment, I stood looking out the window of the room that would have been Ben's. Then I collapsed on the floor in grief. I was stunned. Ben was gone. I felt as though I had just given birth to a stillborn child—one I could not even hold before he was taken from me.

Tears came in floods as I cried out to God, "Why did you tell me it was right for Ben to be part of our family, when he would actually end up going to another family? What about the scriptures I memorized about faith and miracles? I led my husband, children, family, and friends to believe that the miracle would happen. I told them I knew it was right and now it will never happen. Will they ever trust me again?"

Answers to my questions did not come all at once, but over time, I began to understand many principles that were unclear to me before. However, I still don't know all the answers.

This experience prompted many quiet talks, much soul-searching, and an enormous amount of learning among the members of our family. Here is a summary of what we learned:

1. Hope comes from the Holy Ghost. The hope that I had felt while praying for Ben could not have come from the devil. That hope was not meant to deceive me, but to teach me. There are always righteous purposes to be served from our trials.

2. As husbands and wives, we should counsel and pray together and be united on major decisions and spiritual promptings. Those promptings should be pondered in our hearts and shared only when appropriate.

3. Because people have free agency, God's will does not always come to pass; however, his overall purposes are always fulfilled. God allows each of his children the freedom to break the commandments, to ignore the promptings of the Holy Ghost, and to disregard their own consciences. Even though we receive the confirmation of a righteous desire, when the fulfillment of such requires the action or change of heart of another person, we have no guarantee that our desire will come to pass. God always honors his children's free agency. He will never force anyone to do his will, regardless of how good the outcome would be for others. Though we may have a great amount of undoubting faith, God will not deprive anyone of their free agency in order to fulfill someone else's request made in faith.

4. Mortals do not necessarily interpret promptings we receive from God accurately. We know this because he tells us, "My thoughts are not your thoughts." (Isaiah 55:8.) Though I was sure "yes" meant "Yes, it is right for Ben to be part of your family for all eternity." It actually meant, "Yes, it is right for Ben to be an important part of your family (in your thoughts and in your prayers) for three weeks so all of you can learn some vital things. The "yes" may mean it is right for us to work for a goal, not that we will accomplish it. When we receive a confirmation we must not expect God to fulfill our desire the way we want and at the time we want. Nor should we feel that our faith is on trial. We have not necessarily failed if we don't get the exact results we want. *Many* factors are involved—not just our faith. A confirmation

from the Lord does mean "go for it—seeking this goal will bring positive results into your life." Outcomes different from what we expect can sometimes be a delightful surprise.

An experience I had soon after our experience with Ben gave me a beautiful new perspective on the element of surprise that God uses when he fulfills our requests. One Sunday evening I was talking with my daughter, Debbie, about her birthday the following day. There was a knock at the door and two of Debbie's friends, Connie and Amy, came into the house. A few days earlier they had invited Debbie to go shopping for her birthday. She was counting on many happy hours with her friends the next day. Connie was the first to speak, "Debbie, I'm sorry, but Amy and I can't make it tomorrow. We're sorry, but we wanted to stop by tonight to let you know." Trying not to let her disappointment show, Debbie said, "That's okay. Thanks anyway." As the door closed, tears welled up in Debbie's eyes and she bravely tried to hold them back. She looked at me with such sorrow and I held her as she wept. "I wanted to go with them so much . . . it would have been so much fun."

What Debbie did not know was that Amy and Connie had previously asked if I would take Debbie somewhere while they decorated the basement for a big surprise party for her. All of her friends were invited to the party, which was going to be much more fun for her than just a shopping trip with Amy and Connie. As I held Debbie in my arms, I wished I could tell her about the surprise party. I wanted to take away her pain, yet to do so would have deprived her of much of the joy in store for her.

At that moment, I remembered the tears I had wept when I found out I had lost Ben. I had cried to God, "Why did you say that my receiving Ben was right even though he would be taken from me?" I felt a renewal of faith when I realized that, although God had said that working to adopt Ben was a good effort, he had something even greater in store for me which would be revealed later—something that would bring me great joy in the future.

Part of this joy would begin just weeks later as I was called to be Primary president in a ward with over 200 children, a calling I could not have handled if Ben had come into our home. I can now teach *all* these children the gospel. While I was working and praying for Ben, I learned much about children from troubled homes—information that will help me in my new calling.

The faith of every member of our family has been strengthened because of our experience with Ben. We are much less afraid to ask for confirmations of prayers because we know that our faith is strong enough to sustain us while we wait for God to answer in his own time and in his own ways. We no longer demand that requests be answered in our way or that we understand right now. We are better prepared to wait, trust, and believe because we know that God will always help us achieve what is best for us.

Hope and peace cannot be counterfeited by Satan. The Lord will always bless us with good when we pray for righteous desires, even though this blessing may be quite different from what we anticipate. We must also remember that a righteous desire that does not depend on anyone else to bring it about is much different than one that requires the cooperation of other people. It is important to learn to focus more on what we can learn by truly exercising faith than on whether we receive the precise results we desire. When our faith is securely placed in the Lord, and when we do not expect or demand specific results, we can seek the confirmation of a righteous goal and joyfully pursue it with all our hearts, knowing that the outcome (no matter what it is) will be for our best good.

True faith in the Lord is not shaken by adverse circumstances or temporary setbacks. Neither is it shaken when we receive answers different from what we want. The Lord has many good surprises in store for us in the long run if we have the patience and faith to wait on him. As Megan wanted to comfort her daughter about her birthday, the Lord must also long to be able to comfort us in times of bitter disappointment and to tell us about all the good things in store for us. Our struggle is to try to maintain our doubt-not faith in the Savior in spite of disappointment and to always trust in his love and care.

Doubt Not

In spite of all the variables, the Lord requires that we develop doubt-not faith. This is not nearly so hard when we see that it is *Christ* that we must doubt not. We do not doubt his ability to bring to pass all things for our good and to transform all trials into learning experiences. Our faith is based on him, not on getting precise results of every prayer we ask in faith. We can pour all our faith into our belief that he will always have the ultimate triumph and will always make certain that things turn out for our ultimate good. "Ask the Father in my name . . . in faith believing that ye shall receive." (Moroni 7:26). As you read Mark 11:23-24, you will see again that you can ask, and if you have unwavering or undoubting faith, you can receive.

> For verily I say unto you, That whosoever shall say unto this mountain [problem], Be thou removed, and be thou cast into the sea [be solved]; and shall not doubt in his heart, but shall believe that those things which he saith shall come to pass; he shall have whatsoever he saith.

> Therefore I say unto you, What things soever ye desire, when ye pray, believe that ye receive them, and ye shall have them.

To Receive You Must Believe and Doubt Not.

Galatians 6:7 teaches us: "Be not deceived; God is not mocked: for whatsoever a man soweth, that shall he also reap." If we sow believing thoughts, we will receive what we desire. If we sow doubting thoughts, we will reap disappointment.

Since faith is a mental process, it is strengthened by positive inner self-talk and weakened by negative inner self-talk—doubts and fears. If you allow doubting thoughts to enter and stay in your mind, you become double-minded and your faith is weakened. However, if you release each doubting thought, you will be strengthened and your faith will increase.

Weary the Lord until He Blesses You

Luke 18:1 records the Lord's instructions to us: "Men ought always to pray, and not to faint." As I listened to the tapes entitled *Joseph Smith the Prophet*, by Truman Madsen, I noticed an interesting detail—Joseph taught the Saints to "Weary the Lord until he blesses [them]." In Luke 18:1-7 we read the parable of the unjust judge and a widow who, by her continuous importuning, was granted her desire. In verse 5 the unjust judge says: "Yet because this widow troubleth me, I will avenge her lest by her continual coming she weary me."

In verses 6 and 7 the Lord says: "Hear what the unjust judge saith. And shall not God avenge his own elect, which cry day and night unto him, though he bear long with them?"

It appears that if you have faith, evidence of it will be manifested when you are persistent in presenting your righteous desires unto the Lord in prayer until you receive them. If, in the past, you have not received what you asked for from the Lord, perhaps it was because you stopped asking too soon. Remember, our timetable is seldom the same as the Lord's and patience is one of the most important things we can learn. Release your confirmed desire into the Lord's hands and trust in him.

The Lord is pleased when you, by your faith, make it possible for him to help you because you have actively applied the laws of faith. If you do not exercise your faith, the Lord is limited. When you link your faith to his power, all things are possible.

Chapter Six

FAITH SUFFICIENT FOR MIRACLES

DO YOU BELIEVE YOU CAN ACTUALLY HAVE MIRACLES IN YOUR life today? It is no secret—you can! Through unpuzzling the laws of faith and using them, you can catch a glimpse of and start to achieve the beautiful rewards which the Lord holds in store for you, both here and hereafter. You can begin to experience the miracles you would like to have in your life, right here, right now. Through faith, lives are transformed and people experience a joy they have never anticipated or experienced before.

Can faith actually be that strong? Can it produce miracles in my life and yours? We read about miracles in the scriptures and we accept them, but somehow we feel those things could not happen to us today. Yet the people in scripture stories were regular human beings, just as we are. Their miracles came about when they obeyed the laws of faith, just as they can and will for you and me as we learn the laws of faith and put them into practice in our lives.

We, as humans, see a miracle as something beyond the ordinary course of nature, something brought about through the divine intervention of God. We have not understood the part our own faith-thoughts play in bringing about miracles. There have been miracles wrought from the very beginning through faith, and it has only been during times of apostasy and unbelief that miracles have ceased.

Miracles Are Wrought through Faith

If there is no faith, there can be no miracle. The scriptures tell us this many times. Ether 12:12 states that "If there be no faith among the children of men God can do no miracle among them; wherefore, he showed not himself until after their faith."

Mormon Teaches Us about Miracles

As we read the Book of Mormon, we find numerous ways the prophets teach us that miracles are real. Only our unbelief (doubting thoughts and fears) keeps us from receiving them.

Mormon teaches us about miracles in these verses:

> And who shall say that Jesus Christ did not many mighty miracles? And there were many mighty miracles wrought by the hands of the apostles.
>
> And if there were miracles wrought then, why has God ceased to be a God of miracles and yet be an unchangeable Being? And behold, I say unto you he changeth not; if so he would cease to be God; and he ceaseth not to be God, and is a God of miracles.
>
> And the reason why he ceaseth to do miracles among the children of men is because that they dwindle in unbelief and depart from the right way, and know not the God in whom they should trust. (Mormon 9:18-20.)

The prophet Moroni adds his testimony of miracles in the following verses:

> Wherefore, my beloved brethren, have miracles ceased because Christ hath ascended into heaven, and hath sat down on the right hand of God, to claim of the Father his rights of mercy which he hath upon the children of men?
>
> Behold I say unto you, Nay; for it is by faith that miracles are wrought; and it is by faith that angels appear and minister unto men; wherefore, if these things have ceased wo be unto the children of men, for it is because of unbelief, and all is vain. (Moroni 7:27, 37.)

According to these prophets, if we do not accept miracles as part of the experience of life in these days, it is because of a lack of faith, a spirit of unbelief. Have we departed from the right way? Do we not know the God in whom we should trust?

> Behold, when ye shall rend that veil of unbelief which doth cause you to remain in your awful state of wickedness, and hardness of heart, and blindness of mind, then shall the great and marvelous things which have been hid up from the foundation of the world from you—yea, when ye shall call upon the Father in my name, with a broken heart and a contrite spirit, then shall ye know that the Father hath remembered the covenant which he made unto your fathers, O house of Israel.
>
> And then shall my revelations which I have caused to be written by my servant John be unfolded in the eyes of all the people. (Ether 4:15-16.)

We can make this happen when we learn how to use our faith because miracles happen as a result of faith. And we can experience miracles only in answer to our righteous desires, which have been built upon faith, hope, and prayer.

Examples are all around us of people who have experienced the miracles which come when faith is exercised. Let me share a story.

Modern-day Miracles

On Friday 22 August 1933, my father, Sidney Donal Pearce (who went by "Don"), was traveling in his car from Vernal, Utah to the Indian Reservation thirty-five miles away.

Don's mind was occupied with plans for the house he was building in Vernal. All the materials had been delivered to his lot and he planned to start digging the basement the next morning.

When Don was about fourteen miles from LaPoint, a small Utah farming town, he had a most unusual experience. A strong voice spoke to him in his mind saying, "Don, go on a mission."

He was startled, but continued on to his planned destination, thinking all the time of what he had heard. As he visited with the young schoolteacher he planned to marry, he told her about the voice and its message. She was impressed and said, "I would like you better if you *did* go on a mission." He returned to Vernal to his garage apartment about midnight. He spent the night pondering what he should do.

The next morning, at about 5:30 A.M., he went to talk with his bishop, John D. Eaton, who was taking care of early morning chores on his farm. Bishop Eaton told Don he would have called him on a mission already but knew he had no one to pay his way.

Money was scarce during the depression days of the 1930's, but Don had just started supervising the cement work on the Green River bridge in Jensen, Utah. There he did the finishing work for $1.00 an hour and directed all the other workers, who made only $.50 an hour. Because he was making comparatively good wages, he decided he might be able to save enough by November to go on a six-month mission.

After hearing of his experience with the voice, Don's stake president, Hyrum B. Calder, advised him to work and save enough for a two-year mission. However, Don, feeling an urgency in the message he had heard, felt he should leave at least by November.

Don decided to go to his stake patriarch, Fred G. Bingham, and ask for a blessing. Patriarch Bingham told Don in the blessing that the call was from the right source and that he had a special mission and a special work to do.

Bishop Eaton sent in the necessary papers and Don received a call to the Southern States Mission in November. On 6 December he arrived in Atlanta, Georgia, along with nine other Southern States missionaries. The next morning they were taken from their hotel to the chapel, which was close to the mission home. President Callis met them there to interview them. President Charles A. Callis had been mission president of the five Southern States for twenty-five years, but had just been called in the October conference as a new apostle.

President Callis started down the line of the ten elders asking their names, what kind of work they did, and where they were from. Elder Pearce was the last one. President Callis asked, "Elder Pearce, what did you do before you came on your mission?" Don answered, "In a small town, in a small way, I was a contractor and a builder." President Callis immediately looked up from his paperwork and said, "Brother Pearce, you get to Columbia, South Carolina, draw up plans, and build a new church!"

Later, after hearing of the way Don had decided to serve a mission, President Callis, explained to Elder Pearce that he had promised the Saints in Columbia that he would have a chapel built, or started, before he left. He said, "Elder Pearce, I didn't have a missionary in all five states of the mission who knew a thing about building. I still have about five or six weeks left, and the Lord has sent you so I can get that church started before I have to leave."

Faith Precedes the Miracle

Faith precedes the miracle. If there is no faith, there will be no miracle. The scriptures tell us this repeatedly. How then can we make miracles happen in our own lives? There is much to learn about faith and how it works, but you can learn by simply and sincerely praying for more light and knowledge on the laws of faith taught in this book. We can each receive the miraculous results of such personal revelation. It is this personal revelation that our leaders have been teaching us about for years. The prophet and the twelve apostles lead this, the Lord's church, by personal revelation and I honor and follow them. As we become more in tune with the Spirit and build this spirituality into our lives, we will more fully understand the laws of faith with the result that faith will no longer puzzle us. Miracles will begin to happen as we learn to use the laws of faith.

Chapter Seven

THE FAITH/JOY CYCLE

WE HAVE NOW ARRIVED AT THE FAITH/JOY CYCLE—A PRINCIPLE through which you will discover and experience miracles and joy as you follow the laws of faith. Nephi tells us in 2 Nephi 2:25, that "Men are, that they might have joy." This means that you were sent here to learn to find joy! The scriptures teach us repeatedly that through faith you may receive all things and be inspired as to how you can solve each of your problems and challenges. As you experience miracles, you will grow, find greater happiness, and experience joy. That is what the Lord intended.

The chart below shows the Faith/Joy Cycle. Notice how it always starts with your thoughts at the beginning of the cycle. If you follow the cycle through faithfully, you will end up with a feeling of joy. As you repeat the cycle, it builds and strengthens the cycle and builds and strengthens your faith and thus your joy.

You are the most important person you will ever know because only you can develop your own testimony of Jesus Christ. Only you can think the thoughts you have. Only you can learn to release all negative thoughts from your mind and ask the Lord for light and knowledge. Only you can make the choice to follow the Lord Jesus Christ and become pure in heart.

Below the Faith/Joy Cycle, another cycle is depicted: the Depression Cycle. Note that this cycle also begins

The Faith/Joy Cycle

The Lord's System:

Hope→ Faith → Work → Miracle → Joy

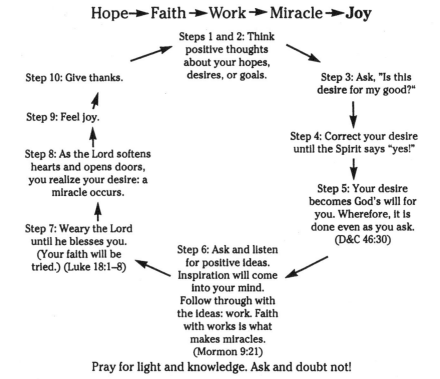

Steps 1 and 2: Think positive thoughts about your hopes, desires, or goals.

Step 10: Give thanks.

Step 9: Feel joy.

Step 8: As the Lord softens hearts and opens doors, you realize your desire: a miracle occurs.

Step 7: Weary the Lord until he blesses you. (Your faith will be tried.) (Luke 18:1–8)

Step 3: Ask, "Is this desire for my good?"

Step 4: Correct your desire until the Spirit says "yes!"

Step 5: Your desire becomes God's will for you. Wherefore, it is done even as you ask. (D&C 46:30)

Step 6: Ask and listen for positive ideas. Inspiration will come into your mind. Follow through with the ideas: work. Faith with works is what makes miracles. (Mormon 9:21)

Pray for light and knowledge. Ask and doubt not!

The Depression Cycle

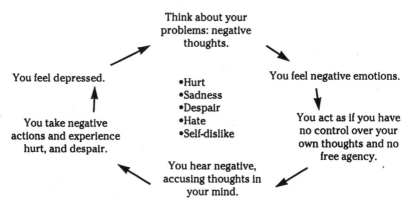

Think about your problems: negative thoughts.

You feel depressed.

You take negative actions and experience hurt, and despair.

•Hurt
•Sadness
•Despair
•Hate
•Self-dislike

You hear negative, accusing thoughts in your mind.

You feel negative emotions.

You act as if you have no control over your own thoughts and no free agency.

Thoughts create emotions which lead to actions. (Mosiah 4:30.)

"If ye have no hope, ye must needs be in despair." (Moroni 10:22.)

with your thoughts. Can you see the implications of these illustrations?

Your Thoughts Determine Your Faith

Your thoughts determine the level of your faith and the amount of joy you will experience. Since you are in charge of your thoughts, you are also in charge of your faith, your miracles, and your joy! There is a natural explanation for the results shown on the chart. Positive thoughts trigger endorphins: natural, positive body chemicals which cause you to experience a natural high. As a result of this high, you then feel a sense of well-being, happy positive emotions, and a joy for life. However, negative thoughts trigger a natural depressant body chemical which causes you to feel sad, negative emotions, which, if not reversed can cause a depression cycle in your life through the body's chemical imbalance.

In Chapter 4, we discussed the fact that thought creates emotion and emotion triggers some type of action from your physical body. This means if you:

—Think positive thoughts about your hopes and goals, you will build faith, experience miracles and joy, and receive answers to prayers.

—Think negative thoughts about your life and your problems, you will experience depression. When this happens, the Lord cannot answer your prayers and you may fall into despair. (See D&C 67:1-3.)

As you learn to watch over your thoughts, releasing and replacing negative thoughts with positive thoughts, your positive experiences will increase along with your faith and joy. For example, when you have ill feelings toward someone, repeat over and over in your mind that you forgive that person. Anytime you realize you are thinking negative thoughts about that person, clear those thoughts from your mind or use the "Would I? Could I? When?" procedure discussed on page 28. Finally, ask the Lord to help you forgive and love that person. By following these steps, you will start to feel forgiveness and love.

These steps will also help you place yourself in control instead of allowing Satan to control your emotions and your life.

Here is another way you can work through a negative situation. You can say, "Father, by my faith in Jesus Christ, I ask thee to take the hurt feelings from me. I choose to release them from my being. Now I joyfully release them and replace them with the Christlike qualities of forgiveness and love. (Word your statements in a way that is right for you and says what you desire.) Then say:

—I forgive myself for allowing negative thoughts in.

—I love myself.

—I love cleansing my inner vessel.

—I love following Jesus Christ.

—I love preparing for Zion.

You can then meditate on the principle of forgiveness for a few moments until you feel the negative feelings leave you. Repeat this as often as needed until you work through each situation and enjoy the miracle of releasing your negative emotions by faith in Jesus Christ.

You can control your thoughts and your emotions when you use this process There is great power in using the name of Jesus Christ in righteous ways.

How to Solve Your Problems and Experience Miracles by Using the Laws of Faith

As you study you will come to understand more and more clearly what the keys to faith are and how to use them. Review the ten steps given on pages 66-68. Your steps may turn out to be a little different. A friend of mine has cut them down to six steps that seem to satisfy her needs. Study the steps. Notice how each of them builds upon and supports the next. Ponder how you could use them in your life.

We, living today, have been given wonderful promises of miracles, both personally and as a people. One of the greatest of these is recorded in Ether 4:7, 11:

And in that day that they shall exercise faith in me,
saith the Lord, even as the brother of Jared did, that they
may become sanctified in me, then will I manifest unto
them the things which the brother of Jared saw, even to
the unfolding unto them all my revelations, saith Jesus
Christ.

But he that believeth these things which I have spoken,
him will I visit with the manifestations of my Spirit, and he
shall know and bear record.

These are not unconditional promises; they are dependent on your faith.

Purify Yourself as the Savior Is Pure

Remember, Satan spoils your miracles by whispering
negative, doubting, evil, fearful, or judgmental thoughts
into your mind. If you are hearing negative words in your
mind, you are tuned into the wrong "radio station."

You cannot have negative or evil thoughts and be in
tune with the Holy Ghost. You must take charge of your
thoughts. You are living here in a physical body but you
are fighting a spiritual battle within your mind and heart.

You are not just a body; you are a spirit intelligence
inside a mortal body. We are told in 1 John 3:2-3 that if you
have the hope of seeing the Savior when he comes, you
must purify yourself, even as the Savior is pure. In order
to do this, you must always watch over your thoughts.

As you learn to use the laws of faith, you will experience more joy in this earthly probation. The way to solve
your problems is by faith. The idea that by faith, all
things are possible, will become a living reality for you.

The faith/joy cycle builds in ever-growing and ever-
widening circles as you repeat it over and over. I believe
that using the ten steps of the faith/joy cycle is one way
the Lord would have us build our faith, solve our daily
challenges, and experience our miracles.

A Missionary Discovers the Laws of Faith

Elder Steven Bush has given me permission to share
his story.

My name is Elder Steven Bush. I am from Farmington, Utah. I have been out in the mission field now for eighteen months (July, 1989) in the Arizona Tempe Mission.

I came to my mission with a great zeal and conviction of the truth of the gospel and the message I was to teach. However, as my mission progressed, I began experiencing doubt, confusion, and negative feelings. I was just not having the success I knew I should have. I was trying to motivate myself but I found that this effort wasn't enough. I knew why I was here, but I didn't really know how to accomplish the huge task of finding and successfully teaching people.

I felt much confusion about how I could grow in faith and become single-minded in order to receive more help from the Lord. I didn't understand how the Spirit speaks to us, either. Answers had come into my mind many times, but I had not recognized this as the way the Lord answers our prayers.

I had been out about four months when President Woolsey called a zone conference in Tucson. He announced that a guest speaker would be speaking on faith.

I was feeling down. I didn't really want to be there. When I heard that the speaker was going to be a woman, I thought, "Oh great! A lady is going to talk to us. What can a woman teach us about missionary work?" That's the male ego for you.

Then she began her talk. "We are all intelligences," she said, "and intelligences think. You talk to yourself seventy-seven percent of your life. You are probably having a mental chit-chat right now." I thought, "Yeah, I am thinking right now all right!" She continued, "You may not know it, but if you are not being as successful as you would like to be, you are being double-minded."

That hit me. It was as though she was talking right to me. I wanted to jump up and say, "I am not being double-minded!" But another voice, deep inside me said, "Yes, you are." It was then that I knew she was speaking truth. I decided maybe I'd better pay close attention to what she had to say. Maybe this was the answer I had been asking for from my Heavenly Father.

As Sister Ringger continued her talk, the Spirit touched my heart and I began to understand how my desire to grow closer to my Heavenly Father could be fulfilled. She discussed our inner self-talk and how we can program the subconscious mind to erase negative thoughts and to replace them with positive thoughts. She spoke of praying for "light and knowledge" to help us find answers and make correct decisions, and also of opening up our inner hearts and minds to listen to the Lord's promptings. She talked about how to grow in faith and become more single-minded in all our missionary work and also in our lives.

These were the answers I needed. I decided I would immediately begin to put them into practice. I wrote up a list of desires I wanted to accomplish and began reciting them to myself each night as I went to bed, etching them into my memory so that my brain-servant would know how I wanted it to work for me.

After I had said my prayers, I repeated in my mind the ten basic goals I had set for myself, beginning with the foundation goal of gaining greater faith in the Lord Jesus Christ. I sincerely repeated over and over to myself these great soul-filling truths:

1. I love Jesus Christ.

2. I know that Jesus Christ lives.

3. I doubt not that he lives.

4. I would do anything for Jesus Christ.

I took the ideas Sister Ringger taught and allowed the Spirit to apply them to me individually. The instructions came into my mind as positive thoughts, and I used them in my own way.

As I adapted the truths to an Elder Bush version, I saw in my mind's eye a kind of computer wheel or disk. Imprinted on the disk I saw only positive thoughts. As the disk went around and around, I continued to focus it on single-minded, positive thoughts. I fed those thoughts into the computer of my mind until good thoughts completely filled it. I pictured that there was no room for negative thoughts so that they would bounce off the disk.

Sometimes, when negative thoughts did come into my mind and affect me, I would dismiss them in the name of Jesus Christ and they would leave.

I was impressed by the Spirit to start praying for light and knowledge about how faith works. When I did, the

Spirit led me to Alma 17:2-4. Alma and the sons of Mosiah met again after serving missions for fourteen years. The brothers told Alma what they did to be successful. Because they had searched the scriptures diligently and had given themselves to much prayer and fasting, they had obtained the spirit of prophecy and revelation. Also, they taught with the power and authority of God.

After reading this, I thought, "If they could do it, I could do it!" I have applied this in all of my missionary efforts since that time, and I have had great success because of it.

When I knocked on people's doors, they often let me in because I knew what I was there for. I knew that Jesus Christ was behind us and that he would help us teach his word in such a way that people would recognize its truth and power.

I prayed for light and knowledge about everything we did. I asked the Lord to lead us to the homes of those who would be willing to hear about the Lord Jesus Christ. I asked him to guide me in the words I should say to them and to prepare the minds of the people so they would be ready to receive our message. I sought always to be open to the promptings of the Spirit.

I taught these truths to my companions. That they also had success brought me great joy.

While in Tucson, we asked in faith for T.V. media referrals to be sent to us so that we could teach the families who sent them in. We committed to the Lord that we would go to each family and teach them as his representatives. Soon, referrals started to arrive—sixty in all. The other missionaries asked me why they didn't receive any. Then I realized what was happening. We had asked for the referrals. We asked and doubted not and our request came to pass.

We took the referrals we received seriously and prayed over each one of them. We placed their names by our bed at night and prayed for the light and knowledge we would need to help them. In the morning we would know what we needed to do for them. What a thrill to be tools in the Lord's hand.

We kept a prayer in our hearts (thoughts) all day, and at people's doorsteps, we would again mentally request light and knowledge to say exactly what the family needed to hear. The ideas were given to us in our minds.

That I should keep stressing how important it is to continue asking for light and knowledge in every situation may appear repetitious, but it works! Our Heavenly Father directed us, and we were successful. Of the sixty referrals we received that month, twenty people were baptized!

Elder Hook, my new companion who came to me in November, also had a great missionary spirit of faith. I taught him the principles of faith I had learned and we prayed for light and knowledge in dealing with all our contacts. That month we taught seventy-three discussions and baptized ten people.

I would like to tell about another experience I had in Tucson. At the time, I was district leader and a couple of companionships were working with some "eternal investigators." These people were doing all the right things—studying the Book of Mormon, praying etc.—but they had not yet committed to baptism. The missionaries didn't know quite what was wrong. I called a district meeting to discuss the situation and to ask for ideas on what we could do to help these people take that necessary step of baptism. The elders and sisters listed many great ideas, but we had tried them all and they hadn't worked.

Then the thought came into my mind that we needed to invite these people to witness a baptism. I challenged the elders and sisters to bring their investigators with them to our next baptism. We could feel the Spirit of the Lord confirm that this was the step which we should take.

My companion and I had scheduled four of our investigators to be baptized the following Sunday. Each of the companionships brought a family of four to the baptism. After the service, each member of those families asked to be baptized that night; they didn't want to wait until the next week. However, since it was 9 P.M., we scheduled their baptismal service for the next day. All eight of the people were baptized! The experience was a real testimony to me of the guidance and promptings of the Spirit.

Later, in December, something happened. I allowed Satan to put doubting thoughts into my mind. I began to think to myself, "Does this really work?" I decided I wanted to experiment. I thought, "I'll just pray for understanding instead of light and knowledge to see if the things I am doing are really right." Of course, that thought was evidence of a doubt. I began to be double-minded again. My attitude changed and everyone noticed, even our investigators. One side effect was that we stopped getting referrals.

December was a terrible month. I had allowed doubt back into my life and all of our work was affected. I did not have the great missionary spirit that I had in previous months. Where had it gone? Without knowing, I had allowed the Spoiler to put doubts in my mind.

January came and I was still feeling depressed. I was then transferred to Globe as district leader. On a transfer day, I was in Mesa getting a free haircut at Martha Johnson's. While I was there, I bumped into Sister Ringger again, which made me reflect upon the principle of praying for light and knowledge and using the law of faith. I realized that the principles of faith had worked and would still work if I used them. Those thoughts motivated me to turn myself around and get back on the right path. I again committed myself to the Lord and started using the principles of faith and prayer and praying for light and knowledge for each of our contacts.

We were out tracting one day and met a family of eight who were Jehovah's Witnesses. I asked for light and knowledge concerning what I could say to them to help them understand. I was told what was needed to awaken them. I could feel the Spirit of the Lord there that day, and we were able to teach them the gospel. Before long, they asked us if they could be baptized. The whole family was baptized into the Church of Jesus Christ of Latter-day Saints.

From time to time, many people have asked me how I have been able to teach and baptize so many people. I have this ability because I do not doubt Jesus Christ. I know that he lives and that through his power, all things are possible. I am human, like everyone else, and I feel that anyone can do this. The key is our "doubt-not faith" that Jesus Christ is the Son of God and that through him, all things are possible. Then, by asking for light and knowledge, positive, pure, enlightening thoughts will come as instructions into the mind, the instrument of the Spirit. Instructions are usually heard in our own tone of voice. We must learn to hear this still, small voice.

Be on guard. Do not even allow yourself to think about negative truths. Fine-tune your thoughts and request light and knowledge and you will be guided. If you ask for angels to be with you to prepare the minds of people you will meet, it will be so. My challenge to you, Brothers and Sisters, is to test and use the methods described here to further develop your faith. These methods require mental effort; the law of faith works through this effort. The law of faith has been brought forth to help us find greater success and to help us become pure in heart in preparation for the Second Coming of Christ.

Understanding the laws of faith has brought great joy, confidence, and strength into my life. I know that I am not alone.

Elder Steven Bush

Taking the Shield of Faith

In D&C 27:15-18 the Lord gives us important instructions to help us withstand Satan:

Wherefore, lift up your hearts and rejoice, and gird up your loins, and take upon you my whole armor, that ye may be able to withstand the evil day, having done all, that ye may be able to stand.

Stand, therefore, having your loins girt about with truth, having on the breastplate of righteousness, and your feet shod with the preparation of the gospel of peace, which I have sent mine angels to commit unto you;

Taking the shield of faith wherewith ye shall be able to quench all the fiery darts of the wicked;

And take the helmet of salvation, and the sword of my Spirit, which I will pour out upon you, and my word which I reveal unto you, and be agreed as touching all things whatsoever ye ask of me, and be faithful until I come, and ye shall be caught up, that where I am ye shall be also. Amen.

The Lord explains here how we may truly be protected from Satan, offering a whole armor, but suggests that the shield of faith is the ultimate protection.

How Do You Do It? Ask for the Shield of Protection.

Sometimes people ask me, "How do you maintain such a joyful attitude? It seems so easy for you." But it has not been easy. I am simply determined that I will have joy. Each day I ask for angels to watch over me and my family. I also ask for a shield of protection from the evil of this world. I envision this shield like a glass dome. It is real, but it is spiritual—something I can see mentally.

I ask for the shield both morning and night in my prayers. I say something like this: "By my faith in Jesus Christ, I ask for a thickened shield of protection, purity, wisdom, charity, and discernment to cover me and my family." Then I ask for angels to be on guard and I request light and knowledge to flow unto me. (See Moroni 7:37.)

The following scriptures can help you as you develop and strengthen your Shield of Protection, which is activated by your faith:

> Finally, my brethren, be strong in the Lord, and in the power of his might.
>
> Put on the whole armour of God, that ye may be able to stand against the wiles of the devil.
>
> For we wrestle not against flesh and blood, but against principalities, against powers, against the rulers of the darkness of this world, against spiritual wickedness in high places.
>
> Wherefore take unto you the whole armour of God, that ye may be able to withstand in the evil day, and having done all, to stand.
>
> Above all, taking the shield of faith, wherewith ye shall be able to quench all the fiery darts of the wicked. (Ephesians 6:10-13, 16.)
>
> For it is by faith that miracles are wrought; and it is by faith that angels appear and minister unto men; wherefore, if these things have ceased wo be unto the children of men, for it is because of unbelief, and all is vain. (Moroni 7:37.)

Finally, when negative thoughts knock on your mental door, use the "Would I? Could I? When?" procedure discussed on page 28.

Through Your Faith in Jesus Christ, You Can Overcome the Wiles of the Devil

This, then, is our challenge: to resist and overcome the temptations of the world and the wiles of the devil.

We will do this as we learn how to use our faith because we know that Jesus Christ lives, and we know how to ask for and receive his help. We can overcome the world. We can use these truths to become pure in heart and to experience miracles as we spread the gospel of Jesus Christ over the earth in preparation for the Millennium.

If great numbers of Latter-day Saints will use their faith in this way, I can see that we will finally be doing something to fulfill this scripture: "And Satan shall be bound that he shall have no place in the hearts of the children of men." (D&C 45:55.)

We are not to be commanded in all things. Now is the time for us to use our own moral agency in a way which will have a great effect on the history of our generation. We can make a difference—perhaps slowly at first—as we spread the truths to family members, other church members, and friends. Then the effects of the application of faith will widen and grow until all who desire will know the laws of faith and will be applying them to achieve miracles in their daily lives.

These ideas on applying the laws of faith and becoming pure in heart are real and doable. By your study of the materials in this book, you can make this great binding of evil occur on an individual basis. How many awakened people will be needed, people who are working daily to be more pure in heart, for us to become like the people of the City of Zion?

Over the last twenty years, wickedness has increased and flooded our land. Only the coming of the Millennium will cleanse the earth of wickedness. We can, however, cleanse our own hearts of wickedness and flood our own lives with faith and its fruits. As many of us do this, we will become a Zion people, pure in heart and prepared to meet the Savior when he comes.

Author's Note:
How the Book Came to Be

I FEEL IT is IMPORTANT TO EXPLAIN THE CIRCUMSTANCES UNDER which the material for this book came into being. I did not deliberately set out to prepare such a plan for publication. Rather, it grew out of asking for and receiving the Lord's help in meeting and mastering particular problems in my life. The materials I present here are not a part of any formal church program, nor are they intended as such. They are simply answers I was given to help me with my own personal problems—answers which worked for me. However, since I originally put the materials together, many others have also found them to be of value. I believe the principles discussed here can help you in your life because they are based on true principles of faith that are found in the scriptures and in messages from our Church leaders. One of the joys of my life is my knowledge that we really do have prophets and apostles in this day to guide us. Our prophets and leaders are teaching us what to do to help us return to God, our Father. I have become aware that prophets teach us what to do, but rarely *how* to do it. Each of us must learn how to receive personal inspiration or revelation from the Lord for ourselves. You will undoubtedly feel the need to adapt the principles that worked for me as you receive your own personal guidance.

The purpose of this book is to share the lessons I have learned that deal with how to listen to the still, small voice, to recognize the impressions of the Spirit, and then to act upon them. The Ten Steps of Faith have helped me realize miracles in my own life. It is my desire that you may find this book to be of value in turning many of your life's challenges into joyous successes.

Before I began to write *Reaching Toward Heaven*, I prayed to gain an increased understanding of faith. I prayed for light and knowledge concerning what faith really was and then studied and pondered. After doing these things, knowledge flowed into my mind and heart.

I began my real search to gain an in-depth understanding of faith by reading an article in the *Ensign* by Elder Ballard. In the article, he explains that Latter-day Saints often lack the faith required to prepare others to be taught the gospel.

I felt sorrow as I read of his concerns because I knew he was correct, that I was one of those members of the Church who often lack the faith needed to help others become interested in the Church. I also recognized a lack of faith on a general level. Each time I read the word faith in the scriptures, I experienced a mental shut-down. I then knew that I needed to ask the Lord in prayer about the kind of faith I was lacking. As I recognized this need because of my past experiences, I then asked for light and knowledge and studied and pondered my questions. At that time, I began to receive understanding. Taking action led to more understanding. In the past, I received light and truth concerning my husband's cancer, the Dead Sea Scrolls, and self-image. Each request for increased light and knowledge opened a flow of information into my life. Blessings flow when we ask for help from the greatest Tutor: the Spirit.

As the laws of faith were made clear to me, my great challenge was to put them on paper; I had very little experience expressing in writing what I could both see in my mind's eye and express vocally in a fireside talk. Again, I would call upon the Lord to send someone to help me organize and write about my impressions on faith. Each time I asked, someone came to help me.

This need for information on faith and improving one's self-image is real. That I have been asked to speak on these concepts to many groups for over eleven years tells me that many people greatly desire to understand how to use faith to bring miracles to pass and thus obtain more joy in their lives. During these eleven years, I have given over 473 talks, averaging forty-three talks per year, to school, civic, and church groups in over ten states and in Mexico and Canada. This demand is evidence to me that people have a need for information on faith and improving self-image.

Our test on the earth basically consists of discerning and choosing good from evil. The fact that different races exist allows us to be tested in certain ways. We must decide whether we will love our brothers and sisters, no matter what their race. While I was in junior high school in southern California, I experienced racial prejudice. I have had to forgive people of other races for their prejudices against me for being white.

When I lived in Hawaii with my family, I learned to love many nationalities of people. Some of these people include Jennie Paul of Tasmania, Australia; Lynn Oaks of New Zealand; Rhoda Lum of Chinese decent; Tiva of Roatonga; Lakalaka Malohifo'ou of Tonga; Tomasi of Fiji; Larry Figueira and his family of Hawaiian, Tahitian, and Filipino decent; and Pam Jones and her family, the Udas (my sister-in-law Diane's family, who have the beauty of Japan in their heritage).

I have talked with Mary Sturlaugson Eyer, author of *A Soul So Rebellious,* about what both of us could do in writing to help people learn to love all others. There is power in this book to help *all* of us to become more discerning as we seek to be a Zion people.

One part of increasing our discernment is overcoming racial prejudices. Those who are pure in heart will have love for people of all nationalities. Satan, the "Spoiler," has the ability to place thoughts in our minds or to "whispereth in [our spiritual] ears," as 2 Nephi 28:22 tells us. At times we are unaware of this because such thoughts come into the mind as if they were our own. As these thoughts develop, even an elect person can be fooled by the body and the mind. We can discern whether the thought is positive (pure and enlightening) or negative (doubting, evil, fearful, or judgmental). One of my purposes in writing this book is to help stop racial prejudice.

I had a number of faith promoting experiences while I was on my mission. I feel a grateful joy when I think about Noel and Wayne McGrevy of Auckland, New Zealand. Acquainting myself with them at CCH opened the door to meet with their parents in their homeland as a missionary. There, my companion and I taught them the gospel. They were sealed in the temple all because the Lord has asked us to go on missions to serve others.

My faith also grew as I worked with George and Ann Davies of Hickurangi, New Zealand. Many years ago, my companion and I sat in her front room and shared our American homemade pumpkin pie. The time we spent together allowed us to become Ann's friends and, eventually, to teach her the gospel of Jesus Christ.

Though missionary work—which involves finding investigators, teaching them, and testifying to them of the restored gospel—is very challenging, I gained greater faith because of this service. I feel deep gratitude to my parents, whose teachings about their mission experiences helped me decide to serve a mission. My faith and joy increased because of this service.

With all of the tests we have on earth, we need light and knowledge so that we can develop and exercise faith. We have the tools and the gift of discernment we need to overcome the evil one. May God bless each of us to increase in faith and fulfill our missions upon the earth. As my mission helped me to increase my faith, I hope this book will help the faith of others to increase.

Carolyn Pearce Ringger

Carolyn has produced many talk tapes and also Alpha-level positive-mind-programming tapes. If you would like more information, call or write:

Carolyn Pearce Ringger
2116 N Morning Star Dr.
Saratoga Springs, Ut 84045

www.faithunpuzzled.com

Carolyn Pearce Ringger

About the Author

Born in Vernal, Utah in 1943, Carolyn moved to Southern California with her family in 1946, where she grew up in the small town of Glen Avon, thirteen miles west of Riverside.

In 1962 the Pearce family moved to Kailua, Hawaii where Carolyn later received her Associate of Arts Degree from the Church College of Hawaii, now called BYU Hawaii. At the age of nineteen, she was the first stake camp director for the Honolulu, Hawaii Stake. Carolyn served in the Auckland, New Zealand Mission in 1965 and 1966.

Carolyn is a widely sought-after speaker. Since 1981, she has produced seven Alpha-level programming tapes in addition to twelve talk tapes and three books. She says that her materials all result from her ability to learn real lessons from life, an ability which results from her desire to know how to do what the prophets teach.

REACHING TOWARD HEAVEN

TEN STEPS FOR ACTIVELY APPLYING FAITH TO SOLVE DAILY PROBLEMS

If you have been thinking "if only I knew how to use my faith to get the help I need," the step-by-step suggestions in this book may bring the breakthrough you most desire. Carolyn Ringger, wanting desperately to exercise faith in her own life, searched the scriptures and the writings of modern prophets for answers. She discovered that faith is not so much something you *have* as something you *do*. Faith is a powerful *action* word.

The author uses scriptures to show how to act on your faith. She also gives ten clear steps for applying faith to problems you face daily—both for concerns that seem small and trivial and for those that seem soul-shattering. She clarifies the principles that will free you to feel the love of the Lord and see his intervention in your life. As you use these principles to reach toward heaven with real intent and a believing heart, you will learn for yourself that miracles have not ceased. The Lord cares for his children as much today as he ever has, and only their doubts and fears stay his hand.

The book points out that one key to activating faith is repentance—cleansing the inner vessel. The exercise of faith creates the desire to repent, and this repentance increases faith. Increased faith then motivates more repentance. These two powerful principles, when put into action, create a wondrous and exciting upward spiral toward the heavenly help you seek.

9 781555 033828

ISBN 1-55503-382-2

Made in the USA
Middletown, DE
12 July 2021